BETTY CROCKER'S
MICROWAVE
COOKING

 **Golden Press New York**
Western Publishing Company, Inc.
Racine, Wisconsin

First Printing, 1977
Copyright © 1977 by General Mills, Inc., Minneapolis, Minnesota.
All rights reserved. Produced in the U.S.A. Library of Congress Catalog Card Number: 77-85234
Golden and Golden Press® are trademarks of Western Publishing Company, Inc.

It wasn't all that long ago that the microwave was looked upon as something of an "abracadabra" kitchen gadget — a speedy thawer of frozen foods, a quick reheater of yesterday's casserole.

But today, microwave cooking has come of age. And no longer is the microwave considered to be a gimmick, but rather an important, meaningful and, to many, even indispensable appliance. While speed may still be its most obvious asset, it offers many other benefits as well. It's cool — the interior never heats up. It's clean — if food should spatter, it can simply be wiped off with a damp cloth. It's convenient — you can heat and serve in the same utensil, be it a casserole, a paper plate or a soup mug. It saves energy — and because food is prepared so quickly, little or nothing "cooks away."

It stands to reason, then, that the more you use your microwave, the more you will enjoy its many benefits and the more it will lighten your everyday cooking chores. And that's the purpose of this book. In it you will find the kinds of recipes you've always enjoyed—but especially adapted to the speed and ease of microwaving. So there's no reason to change your menus just to suit a new method of cooking. We think you'll be delighted with the new-found nuances of Sweet 'n Sour Pork and Seafood Newburg, with the tender crispness of Orange-buttered Carrots, with the extra-light touch that's brought to Banana-topped Cake. Included, too, are Sugar-baked Apples, Pecan Tarts and other desserts as well as recipes for soups, sandwiches and snacks. And every recipe has been tested in the Betty Crocker Kitchens and in homes across the country.

As you use these recipes, we hope you will discover that microwaving is as versatile and exciting as it is clean, cool and quick. Enjoy it . . . and your new-found time.

Betty Crocker

CONTENTS

THE WHYS AND WHEREFORES

There's more to microwave cooking than pushing a button. And like anything new, it takes some getting used to. Microwave cooking is not just a matter of cooking a faster way; it's cooking in a new and different way. It calls for a certain sense of adventure — a willingness to experiment with your favorite recipes on a trial-and-error basis and to change some of your long-established cooking habits and techniques. Once you understand the principles of microwave cooking — the basic whys and wherefores — you'll be able to get more use out of the recipes in this book . . . and out of your own microwave.

MICROWAVES — HOW THEY WORK

There's nothing magical about microwaves. They are simply electromagnetic waves of energy, very similar to radio and television waves. The magnetron tube converts regular electricity into microwaves. These microwaves, which are deflected by metal, bounce off the walls, floor and ceiling of the interior in an irregular pattern.

But when they encounter any matter containing moisture — specifically food — they are absorbed into it. (A stirrer fan further deflects the microwaves so that they penetrate the food from all sides.) The microwaves agitate and vibrate the moisture molecules at such a great rate that friction is created; the friction, in turn, creates heat and the heat causes the food to cook. (In conventional cooking methods, heat is applied **to** the food; with microwave cooking, heat is generated **within** the food. Unlike a conventional oven, the microwave never heats up.) Because microwaves only go about 1 inch into the food, the additional heating or cooking occurs by conduction and/or convection. It is this same conduction that heats the dishes that hold the food — so do remember to use hot pads.

UTENSILS

The best utensils for microwave cooking are those that permit the microwaves to pass right through them and into the food. Although there are many specially developed "microwave-suitable" products on the market, chances are you have plenty of utensils on hand.

⊡ Glassware is very well suited to microwave heating and cooking. It's best to use oven-tempered glass for cooking. Remember, cooked food does become very hot, and that heat is transferred to the utensil; thus, the material must be strong enough to withstand high temperatures.

⊡ Paper is another good material to use for the brief heating of many different types of food. It is especially good to use when reheating rolls, muffins and the like. For cooking, use more durable paper products or containers designed for microwaving.

⊡ Dishwasher-safe plastic containers can also be used for quick reheatings. They are not recommended for cooking, however, as the hot food can distort and even melt the plastic. The plastic cooking pouches that contain frozen vegetables and entrées can withstand very high temperatures and may be used successfully in a microwave. Just make a slit in the pouch to allow for the escape of steam. There are also a wide variety of plastic cooking dishes, muffin pans and racks available for microwave use.

⊡ Ceramic plates and casseroles are microwave-safe if they contain no metals. However, many varieties of clay and claylike compositions may have traces of metal; so if you are in doubt, test them. To test any dish, place 1 cup water in a glass measure in the microwave on or beside the dish. Microwave 1 minute on the 100% setting. If the dish becomes warm, it should not be used for microwaving.

⊡ China can also be used in the microwave. Just be sure there are no metal decorations or trims to deflect the microwaves. Strangely enough, a tiny fleck of gold, silver or other metal can cause "arcing" and do more damage than a larger all-metal utensil.

⊡ Metal utensils should not be used in microwave cooking. Microwaves cannot penetrate metal; rather, they are deflected by it. However, some manufacturers suggest using small pieces of aluminum foil to shield areas that might otherwise tend to overcook (for example, the wing tips on a chicken or the corners of a cake baked in a square pan), some even allow the use of TV-dinner trays. Be sure to follow your manufacturer's recommendations.

WATCH THE TIME

Timing recipes tends to be a little tricky in a microwave — there are more variables than you might expect. When converting a favorite recipe to the microwave method, find a similar recipe in the instruction book that came with your oven or in this book and use it as your guide. When trying a recipe for the first time, always cook it to the minimum side if a time range is given. If underdone, you can always cook it a bit longer. Why these cautions?

⊡ The density of food has a bearing on the cooking time. Porous foods such as breads and cakes heat or cook very quickly, while dense foods such as roasts and casseroles call for longer cooking times.

⊡ Starting temperatures can also make a difference. The colder the food, the longer the time required to heat or cook it. (For testing the recipes in this book, foods normally stored at room temperature were used at that temperature, while foods normally stored in the refrigerator were prepared at that storage temperature.)

⊡ The quantity of food is another factor. For any given microwave setting, there is always the same number of microwaves available for heating or cooking. If only one item is in the oven, all the microwaves are concentrated on that single item. If there are more items in the oven, the microwaves must be shared and the concentration on each item is reduced, thus increasing the time required to heat or cook. Keep this point in mind if you cook for a family of hearty eaters. With certain recipes, the microwave method may offer no saving in time.

TO COVER OR NOT TO COVER

Coverings are often used to keep the moisture in and to prevent liquid foods from spattering. When using the recipes in this book, be aware of the following terminology:

⊡ "Cover" means that no steam or moisture should escape. If using a casserole, use its matching lid or, lacking that, rest a plate on top. If using a utensil with an odd shape, cover the top with plastic wrap, sealing it all the way around.

⊡ "Cover tightly" is used in recipes calling for utensils that normally do not have fitted covers.

⊡ "Cover loosely" means that a certain amount of moisture and steam should be permitted to escape from the food. If using a casserole, put the lid on slightly ajar. With other utensils, such as baking dishes, glass measures or bowls, cover with a sheet of waxed paper, a paper towel or use plastic wrap with the corners turned back.

THE SHAPE OF THINGS

Be willing to see things a little differently. In microwave cooking, the more surface that is exposed, the faster and more evenly the food will cook.

⊡ Place thicker pieces of meat toward the sides of the dish, the bonier parts toward the center. Arrange the blossom ends of broccoli in the center, with the stalks radiating out to the sides.

⊡ If heating several items on a plate — sweet rolls, for example — arrange them in a circle. And don't place one in the center.

⊡ A circle shape is almost ideal for microwave cooking. It's even better if the circle is a ring, eliminating the slower-to-cook center altogether. This shape is used for many cakelike desserts as well as for some meat dishes. There are a number of glass, ceramic and plastic ring dishes on the market, but you can improvise by putting a straight-sided beverage glass in the center of a bowl or casserole. The circle shape eliminates corners, which, with certain types of

NOTE

All the recipes in this book were developed and tested in countertop microwaves with wattage output ratings of 600 to 700 watts. A variety of makes and models were used and, although they had different features and power levels, all recipes were tested using 100% settings — High, Full or Number 10. The timing and cooking techniques outlined for each recipe will give optimum results when this full power setting is used. If your microwave has a wattage output rating of less than 600 watts, you will find that some increase in the suggested cooking time may be necessary.

food, tend to overcook because of the heavy concentration of microwaves at the outer edges.

SPECIAL TWISTS

Because the microwaves bounce around the oven cavity in random patterns, foods often cook faster in one area of the oven, or even in one area of a baking dish, than in another. Thus it is sometimes necessary to rotate the dish, rearrange food, stir it or even to let it stand for a while in order to even out the cooking.

⊡ Turn dishes one-quarter or one-half turn midway through the cooking period as directed or when necessary.

⊡ Stirring helps even out the cooking for many sauces and casserole-like dishes. Always stir from the outside edges (where the food is hotter) into the center. Foods that can be stirred usually do not require rotating or standing.

⊡ A "standing time" after cooking allows the heat in the food to equalize. Standing times are also used when a food is heating or cooking more quickly than desired.

IT'S TODAY'S WAY

The speed, ease and convenience of microwave cooking are tailored to today's way of life. And it's up to you to decide just how and when this new method of cooking can help you get more out of — or, perhaps, into — your own life.

The recipes on the following pages have been specially chosen to show you how microwave cooking can come to the fore in preparing your daily meals. These are the types of foods you like to prepare for your family; they're the types of foods your family likes to eat.

And while you are exploring the world of microwave cooking, we also hope you will take a tip from our serving recommendations and discover a healthier way of eating. Though these servings may seem small at first glance, each portion has been carefully checked for its protein adequacy.

Speedier cooking. Healthier eating. Two good ideas for today.

MAIN DISHES

BEEF STROGANOFF

1 tablespoon vegetable oil
1 pound boneless beef sirloin steak, cut into thin strips
8 ounces fresh mushrooms, sliced
1 medium onion, sliced
¼ cup water
2 tablespoons flour
1 teaspoon dry mustard
1 teaspoon salt
¼ teaspoon pepper
1 cup dairy sour cream
2 cups hot cooked rice or noodles

Stir oil and meat in 2-quart casserole until beef is coated. Cover and microwave until meat is no longer pink, 4½ to 5 minutes. Remove meat from casserole; reserve meat and juices.

Add mushrooms and onion to meat juices. Cover and microwave until mushrooms are tender, 5 to 6 minutes.

Shake water and flour in tightly covered jar; stir into mushrooms. Sprinkle with dry mustard, salt and pepper. Microwave uncovered to boiling, 30 seconds. Boil until thickened, 1 minute.

Stir in reserved meat, then sour cream. Microwave uncovered until hot, about 1 minute. Serve over rice or noodles.

4 servings.

ORIENTAL BEEF AND PEA PODS

1 small head cauliflower
1 green pepper, cut into strips
1 pound beef round steak or tenderloin tip, cut into paper-thin strips, about 3 inches long
1 clove garlic, minced
1 medium onion, chopped
3 tablespoons soy sauce
1 package (6 ounces) frozen pea pods
2 cups water
¼ cup cornstarch
4 teaspoons instant beef bouillon
½ teaspoon sugar
3 cups hot cooked rice

Break cauliflower into flowerets; cut each into ¼-inch slices. Combine cauliflower, green pepper, beef, garlic and onion in 2-quart casserole. Drizzle with soy sauce; stir lightly to coat evenly. Cover and microwave 6 minutes; stir. Cover and microwave until meat is no longer pink, 3 to 5 minutes.

Add frozen pea pods. Cover and microwave until pea pods are thawed, 2 to 3 minutes.

Mix water, cornstarch, bouillon and sugar in 4-cup glass measure. Stir in juices from meat. Microwave 2½ minutes; stir. Microwave to boiling, 2 to 3 minutes. Stir into meat mixture. Serve over rice.

4 to 6 servings.

QUICK BEEF STEW

2 to 2½ cups cut-up cooked beef (about 1 pound)
4 medium carrots, cut into 2½-inch strips
3 medium potatoes, pared and cut into 1½-inch pieces
1 cup sliced celery
1 envelope (1⅜ ounces) onion soup mix
3 tablespoons flour
2¼ cups water

Mix all ingredients in 2½-quart casserole. Cover and microwave to boiling, 10 to 12 minutes; stir. Cover and let stand 5 minutes. Microwave until vegetables are tender, 10 to 12 minutes, stirring every 5 minutes.

4 to 6 servings.

DRIED BEEF AND NOODLE CASSEROLE

4 ounces dried beef, snipped into small pieces
1 cup water
1 small onion, chopped
2 cups uncooked noodles
1 can (10¾ ounces) condensed cream of mushroom soup
½ cup milk
1 cup water
1 teaspoon dried parsley flakes
1 cup shredded Cheddar cheese (about 4 ounces)

Cover and microwave dried beef and 1 cup water in 2-quart casserole to boiling, 2 to 3 minutes; drain.

Stir in onion, noodles, soup, milk, water and parsley flakes. Cover and microwave 10 minutes; stir. Cover and microwave until noodles are tender, 5 to 6 minutes.

Stir in cheese. Cover and microwave until melted, 2 to 3 minutes.

5 or 6 servings.

RAVIOLI BAKE

1 can (15 ounces) beef ravioli in sauce
1 can (4 ounces) mushroom stems and pieces, drained
3 green onions, sliced
½ cup shredded mozzarella cheese
¼ teaspoon Italian seasoning
¼ teaspoon garlic salt
¼ cup croutons, crushed

Mix all ingredients except croutons in 1-quart casserole or bowl. Sprinkle croutons over top. Cover loosely and microwave until ravioli mixture is hot, 4½ to 5½ minutes.

3 or 4 servings.

HAMBURGER PATTIES

1 pound hamburger
1 small onion, chopped
1 slice bread, cubed
2 tablespoons catsup
½ teaspoon salt
1½ teaspoons prepared mustard
1 teaspoon Worcestershire sauce
1 teaspoon prepared horseradish

Mix all ingredients. Shape into 4 patties, about 3½ inches in diameter. Place in square baking dish, 8 x 8 x 2 inches. If desired, brush each patty with additional catsup. Cover loosely and microwave 5 minutes; turn dish one-quarter turn. Microwave until done, 2 to 3 minutes.

4 patties.

NOTE: Because germs can get mixed into ground beef during preparation, it should be thoroughly cooked, until all trace of pink disappears.

VEGETABLE-FILLED PATTIES

1   pound lean hamburger
½   cup dry bread crumbs
¼   cup finely chopped onion
1   egg
1   teaspoon salt
⅛   teaspoon pepper
1   can (10¾ ounces) condensed cream of
    mushroom soup
½   can (3-ounce size) French fried onions
1   can (16 ounces) French-style green beans,
    drained
½   teaspoon Worcestershire sauce

Mix hamburger, bread crumbs, chopped onion, egg, salt, pepper and ⅓ of the soup. Shape into 6 oval patties. Place in oblong baking dish, 12 x 7½ x 2 inches. Depress center of each patty, forming a ½-inch rim around edge.

Reserve a few French fried onions for garnish. Mix remaining onions with beans, Worcestershire sauce and remaining soup; spoon into center of each patty. Cover loosely and microwave 4 minutes; turn dish one-half turn. Microwave until meat is done, 8 to 10 minutes. Garnish with reserved onions.

6 servings.

MEATBALLS

1   pound hamburger
1   small onion, chopped
2   slices bread, cubed
1   egg
¼   cup milk
1   teaspoon salt
1   teaspoon Worcestershire sauce
⅛   teaspoon pepper

Mix all ingredients. Shape into 12 meatballs, about 2 inches in diameter. Place in baking dish, 8 x 8 x 2 inches. Cover loosely and microwave 4 minutes; rearrange meatballs. Cover and microwave until meatballs are done, 3 to 4 minutes; drain.

12 meatballs.

SWEET-SOUR MEATBALLS

    Meatballs (above)
2   tablespoons cornstarch
1   can (15¼ ounces) pineapple chunks
½   cup chopped green pepper
½   cup packed brown sugar
¼   cup vinegar
1   tablespoon soy sauce

Prepare and microwave Meatballs. Mix cornstarch and pineapple (with syrup) in 4-cup glass measure. Stir in green pepper, brown sugar, vinegar and soy sauce. Microwave 2 minutes; stir. Microwave to boiling, 1½ minutes. Boil until thickened and translucent, 2½ to 3½ minutes.

Pour sauce over meatballs. Microwave uncovered until meatballs are hot, 4 to 5 minutes.

4 to 6 servings.

FAMILY MEAT LOAF

1½ cups herb-seasoned stuffing mix
⅔ cup milk
1½ pounds hamburger
 1 small onion, chopped
 1 egg
 1 teaspoon salt
¼ teaspoon pepper

Pour milk over stuffing cubes. Mix in remaining ingredients. Press evenly into loaf dish, 9 x 5 x 3 inches. Cover loosely and microwave 10 minutes; turn loaf dish one-half turn. Microwave until meat is set in center, 5 to 6 minutes.

4 to 6 servings.

CHEESE-FILLED MEAT LOAF

 1 pound lean hamburger
⅔ cup dry bread crumbs
 1 can (10½ ounces) pizza sauce
 1 egg
 1 medium onion, chopped
 1 teaspoon salt
⅛ teaspoon garlic powder
 1 carton (12 ounces) small curd cottage cheese
 1 can (4 ounces) mushroom stems and pieces, drained
 1 tablespoon dried parsley flakes
¾ teaspoon Italian seasoning
 1 egg

Mix hamburger, bread crumbs, ½ cup of the pizza sauce, 1 egg, the onion, salt and garlic powder; reserve. Mix remaining ingredients for cheese filling.

Press ⅓ of the meat mixture in bottom of oblong baking dish, 10 x 6 x 1½ inches. Spread cheese filling over meat. Spoon remaining meat mixture onto top; spread to cover filling. Cover loosely and microwave 10 minutes; turn dish one-quarter turn. Microwave until meat is firm in center, about 7 minutes. Let stand 5 minutes before cutting.

Microwave remaining pizza sauce in dish to boiling, 1 to 2 minutes; serve over Meat Loaf.

8 servings.

MEXICAN PIZZA

 2 tablespoons cornmeal
 2 cups biscuit baking mix
½ cup water
 1 pound hamburger
½ cup water
 1 envelope (1¼ ounces) taco seasoning mix
 1 can (16 ounces) refried beans
 1 cup shredded Cheddar cheese (about 4 ounces)
 1 medium onion, sliced
 1 tomato, chopped
    Taco sauce (optional)

Cut a 12-inch circle from cardboard. Cut a waxed paper circle the same size and place on cardboard circle. Sprinkle with cornmeal.

Mix biscuit mix and ½ cup water until a soft dough forms. Gently smooth dough into a ball on lightly floured surface. Knead 5 times. Roll to 13-inch circle. Transfer to waxed paper circle. Turn edge of dough under and pinch to form a rim. Microwave uncovered 3 minutes; turn cardboard one-quarter turn. Microwave until crust is no longer doughy, 2 to 4 minutes.

Crumble hamburger into 1-quart casserole. Microwave uncovered until meat is firm, 5 to 6 minutes. Stir to break up meat; drain. Stir in ½ cup water and the taco mix. Microwave uncovered until thickened, 5 to 6 minutes.

Spread refried beans over crust; top with meat mixture. Sprinkle with cheese and onion. Microwave uncovered until cheese is melted, 3 to 4 minutes. Sprinkle with chopped tomato and drizzle with taco sauce.

6 servings.

HAMBURGER STROGANOFF CASSEROLE

1 pound hamburger
1 medium onion, chopped
1 clove garlic, minced
2½ cups uncooked noodles
2 teaspoons instant beef bouillon
½ teaspoon dry mustard
½ teaspoon salt
 Dash of pepper
1 can (4 ounces) mushroom stems and pieces
¼ cup dry white wine or water
2 tablespoons tomato paste
2 cups water
¾ cup dairy sour cream

Crumble hamburger into 2-quart casserole; add onion and garlic. Microwave uncovered until meat is firm, 5 to 6 minutes. Stir to break up meat; drain.

Stir in noodles, bouillon, mustard, salt, pepper, mushrooms (with liquid), wine, tomato paste and water. Cover and microwave until mixture boils and noodles are tender, 11 to 13 minutes, stirring every 4 minutes. Stir in sour cream. Let stand uncovered 5 minutes.

4 to 6 servings.

HAMBURGER PIE ITALIANO

1 pound hamburger
1 egg
2 tablespoons dry bread crumbs
1 teaspoon salt
1 teaspoon Italian seasoning
¼ teaspoon pepper
1 can (6 ounces) tomato paste
1 small green pepper, sliced
1 cup shredded mozzarella cheese (about 4 ounces)
1 teaspoon dried oregano leaves

Crumble hamburger into 1-quart casserole. Microwave uncovered 3 minutes; stir.

Microwave uncovered until meat is firm, 2 to 3 minutes. Stir to break up meat finely; drain.

Stir in egg, bread crumbs, salt, Italian seasoning and pepper. Press in bottom and up side of 9-inch pie plate. Microwave uncovered until meat is set, 4½ to 5½ minutes.

Spread tomato paste over meat; top with green pepper, cheese and oregano. Microwave uncovered until cheese is melted, 2 to 3 minutes. Cut into wedges.

5 or 6 servings.

TOP HAT STUFFED PEPPERS

5 green peppers
1 pound hamburger
¼ cup chopped celery
1 cup quick-cooking rice
⅓ cup catsup
2 tablespoons chopped onion
1 tablespoon Worcestershire sauce
½ teaspoon salt
⅛ teaspoon garlic powder
 Dash of pepper
1 egg
1 can (8 ounces) tomato sauce
1 teaspoon sugar
¼ teaspoon dried basil leaves

Cut thin slice from stem end of each pepper. Remove all seeds and membranes; wash inside and out.

Mix hamburger, celery, rice, catsup, onion, Worcestershire sauce, salt, garlic powder, pepper and egg. Fill peppers with meat mixture. Place in square baking dish, 8 x 8 x 2 inches. Cover loosely and microwave until meat is firm, 10 to 12 minutes.

Mix tomato sauce, sugar and basil in 2-cup glass measure. Microwave to boiling, 2 to 3 minutes. Serve sauce over peppers.

5 servings.

HAMBURGER-RICE HOT DISH

    5 slices bacon
    1 pound hamburger
    1 medium onion, chopped
    ½ cup chopped green pepper
    1 can (16 ounces) stewed tomatoes
    1 cup uncooked long grain rice
    2 cups water
 1¼ teaspoons salt
    1 teaspoon chili powder
    ⅛ teaspoon pepper

Layer bacon between paper towels in 2-quart casserole. Microwave until crisp, 4 to 6 minutes. Remove bacon and paper towels.

Crumble hamburger into casserole; add onion and green pepper. Microwave uncovered until meat is firm, 5 to 6 minutes. Stir to break up meat; drain.

Crumble bacon; add to meat along with remaining ingredients. Cover and microwave to boiling, 8 to 10 minutes. Stir and let stand, covered, 10 minutes. Microwave until rice is tender, 12 to 16 minutes. Let stand 5 minutes.

6 servings.

ONE-DISH SPAGHETTI CASSEROLE

    1 pound hamburger
    1 medium onion, chopped
    ½ cup chopped celery
    1 can (28 ounces) whole tomatoes
    1 can (4 ounces) mushroom stems and pieces, drained
 1½ cups water
    1 teaspoon salt
    ½ teaspoon garlic salt
    1 package (7 ounces) thin spaghetti, broken into 3-inch pieces
       Grated Parmesan cheese (optional)

Crumble hamburger into 3-quart casserole; add onion and celery. Microwave uncovered until meat is firm, 5 to 6 minutes. Stir to break up meat; drain.

Stir tomatoes (with liquid), mushrooms, water and salts into meat mixture. Cover and microwave 5 minutes.

Stir in spaghetti. Cover and microwave until spaghetti is tender, 15 to 17 minutes, stirring every 5 minutes. Let stand 5 minutes. Sprinkle with cheese.

6 servings.

BEEF AND BEANS WITH CORN BREAD TOPPING

    ¾ pound hamburger
    1 medium onion, chopped
    1 can (16 ounces) pork and beans in tomato sauce
    ½ cup barbecue sauce
    ½ teaspoon salt
       Corn Bread Topping (below)

Crumble hamburger into 2-quart casserole; add onion. Microwave uncovered until meat is firm, 5 to 6 minutes. Stir to break up meat; drain. Stir in pork and beans, barbecue sauce and salt. Cover and microwave to boiling, 3 to 4 minutes.

Prepare Corn Bread Topping. Spoon onto meat mixture, forming a ring of corn bread around side of dish. (Topping will cook toward center.) Microwave uncovered 2 minutes; turn dish one-quarter turn. Microwave until topping is no longer doughy, 2 to 3 minutes.

5 servings.

CORN BREAD TOPPING
    ½ cup biscuit baking mix
    ¼ cup yellow cornmeal
    2 teaspoons sugar
    ⅛ teaspoon salt
    2 teaspoons vegetable oil
    1 egg, slightly beaten
    ¼ cup milk

Mix all ingredients until well blended.

UPSIDE-DOWN MEAT PIE

1 pound hamburger
½ cup chopped celery
1 medium onion, chopped
1 can (10¾ ounces) condensed tomato soup
1 teaspoon Worcestershire sauce
½ teaspoon salt
⅛ teaspoon pepper
2 eggs
½ package (10-ounce size) frozen peas (1 cup)
1½ cups biscuit baking mix
½ cup water
¼ cup grated Parmesan cheese

Crumble hamburger into 2-quart casserole, about 9 inches in diameter; add celery and onion. Microwave uncovered until meat is firm, 5 to 6 minutes. Stir to break up meat; drain. Stir in soup, Worcestershire sauce, salt, pepper, eggs and frozen peas. Cover and microwave 5 minutes; stir. Microwave uncovered until hot and bubbly, 3 minutes.

Mix biscuit mix, water and cheese. Spoon onto hot meat mixture, spreading to cover. Microwave uncovered 3 minutes; turn dish one-quarter turn. Microwave until topping is no longer doughy, 2 to 3 minutes. Spoon or invert onto serving plate and cut into wedges.

5 or 6 servings.

ENCHILADA CASSEROLE

1 pound hamburger
1 medium onion, chopped
1 green pepper, chopped
1 can (8 ounces) tomato sauce
1 can (10 ounces) enchilada sauce
1 can (15 ounces) pinto beans
6 six-inch tortillas
1 medium tomato, chopped
½ cup shredded Cheddar cheese (about 2 ounces)

Crumble hamburger into 1½-quart casserole. Add onion and green pepper. Microwave uncovered until meat is firm, 5 to 6 minutes. Stir to break up meat; drain.

Stir in tomato sauce, enchilada sauce and beans (with liquid). Cover and microwave to boiling, 3 to 4½ minutes.

Spoon 2 cups meat sauce into oblong baking dish, 12 x 7½ x 2 inches. Place ¼ cup remaining meat sauce in center of each tortilla. Fold sides of tortilla up over filling, overlapping edges. Place tortillas seam sides down in baking dish. Spoon remaining sauce over tortillas. Cover loosely and microwave until hot, 9 to 10 minutes.

Sprinkle tomato in strip down center of casserole; sprinkle cheese on each side. Microwave uncovered until cheese is melted, 2 to 3 minutes.

6 servings.

GLAZED PORK LOIN ROAST

2- to 2½-pound fresh pork boneless loin roast
1 clove garlic, cut into fourths
1 teaspoon salt
1 tablespoon orange marmalade
1 teaspoon prepared mustard
½ teaspoon dried thyme leaves

Make 4 slits in fat on pork roast with tip of sharp knife; insert a piece of garlic in each slit. Sprinkle roast with salt. Place fat side down on microwave roasting rack or inverted saucer in oblong baking dish, 12 x 7½ x 2 inches. Cover loosely and microwave 12 minutes; turn roast fat side up. Cover tightly and let stand 10 minutes. Microwave 5 minutes.

Mix marmalade, mustard and thyme; spread on roast. Cover loosely and microwave until roast is done (170°), 5 to 7 minutes.

8 to 10 servings.

ORIENTAL PORK

2 cups ¼-inch strips cooked fresh pork (about 1 pound)
½ cup water
½ cup orange juice
¼ teaspoon salt
Dash of pepper
3 tablespoons soy sauce
1 can (8 ounces) water chestnuts, drained and sliced
1 can (16 ounces) bean sprouts, drained
2 cups thinly sliced Chinese cabbage
1 tablespoon cornstarch
1 tablespoon water
3 cups hot cooked rice

Combine pork, ½ cup water, the orange juice, salt, pepper and soy sauce in 2-quart casserole. Cover and microwave 10 minutes.

Stir in water chestnuts, bean sprouts and cabbage. Cover and microwave until cabbage is tender, 3 to 4 minutes.

Blend cornstarch and 1 tablespoon water in 2-cup glass measure. Drain juices from meat mixture into cornstarch mixture; stir well.

Microwave until mixture boils and thickens slightly, 2 to 3 minutes. Pour over meat and vegetables. Serve over rice.

5 servings.

SWEET 'N SOUR PORK

1½ pounds boneless fresh pork, cubed
1 medium onion, sliced
1 can (8 ounces) pineapple chunks
¼ cup packed brown sugar
3 tablespoons cornstarch
2 tablespoons lemon juice
1 tablespoon soy sauce
½ teaspoon salt
⅛ teaspoon pepper
⅛ teaspoon ground ginger
1 small green pepper, cut into 1-inch pieces
1 package (6 ounces) frozen pea pods

Mix pork, onion, pineapple (with syrup), brown sugar, cornstarch, lemon juice, soy sauce, salt, pepper and ginger in 2-quart casserole. Cover and microwave 5 minutes; stir. Cover and microwave until meat is done, 8 to 10 minutes.

Stir in green pepper and pea pods. Cover and microwave 2½ minutes; stir. Cover and microwave until green pepper and pea pods are tender, 3 to 4 minutes.

4 or 5 servings.

CHEESY PORK AND CABBAGE

1   to 1½ pounds boneless fresh pork, cubed
1   can (11 ounces) condensed Cheddar
    cheese soup
3   to 4 medium carrots, shredded
1   teaspoon packed brown sugar
1   teaspoon salt
¼   teaspoon caraway seed
⅛   teaspoon pepper
1   teaspoon vinegar
1   small head cabbage, shredded (5 cups)

Cover and microwave pork in 2½-quart casserole until meat is no longer pink, 8 to 10 minutes. Stir in soup, carrots, brown sugar, salt, caraway seed, pepper and vinegar. Cover and microwave to boiling, 5 to 6 minutes.

Add cabbage. Cover and microwave until meat and cabbage are tender, 12 to 15 minutes, stirring every 5 minutes.

5 or 6 servings.

PORK CHOPS ON STUFFING

1   package (6 ounces) chicken-flavored
    stuffing mix
2   eggs, beaten
1   can (10¾ ounces) condensed cream of
    mushroom soup
1   teaspoon instant chicken bouillon
1   cup water
6   fresh pork loin chops (about 2 pounds),
    about ½ inch thick
½   cup milk
1   tablespoon chopped pimiento

Stir stuffing mix (with seasoning packet), eggs, half of the soup, the bouillon and water in baking dish, 12 x 7½ x 2 inches. Arrange chops on stuffing. Mix milk, pimiento and remaining soup; pour over chops.

Cover loosely and microwave 15 minutes; turn dish one-half turn. Microwave until chops are done, 8 to 10 minutes.

5 or 6 servings.

BARBECUED PORK CHOPS

6   fresh pork rib chops (about 1½ pounds),
    about ½ inch thick
1   teaspoon salt
½   teaspoon pepper
1   small onion, sliced
¼   cup maple-flavored syrup
¼   cup catsup
½   teaspoon Worcestershire sauce
¼   teaspoon prepared mustard
    Dash of ground cloves

Sprinkle pork chops with salt and pepper. Place in square baking dish, 8 x 8 x 2 inches. Top with onion slices. Cover loosely and microwave 10 minutes. Turn and rearrange chops; drain.

Mix syrup, catsup, Worcestershire sauce, mustard and cloves; pour over chops. Cover tightly and microwave until chops are done, 10 to 12 minutes.

6 servings.

ITALIAN PORK CHOP BAKE

1   jar (15½ ounces) spaghetti sauce
1⅔ cups water
¾   cup uncooked long-grain rice
1½ teaspoons instant chicken bouillon
¾   teaspoon salt
⅛   teaspoon pepper
½   cup sliced ripe olives
1   small onion, sliced
6   fresh pork loin chops (about 2 pounds),
    about ½ inch thick

Mix all ingredients except pork chops in oblong baking dish, 12 x 7½ x 2 inches. Cover loosely and microwave 5 minutes.

Arrange chops on top, pushing them into sauce. Cover loosely and microwave 15 minutes. Turn and rearrange chops; stir rice. Cover tightly and microwave until chops and rice are done, 10 to 15 minutes.

6 servings.

PORK RIBS AND SAUERKRAUT

2 pounds fresh pork country-style ribs
1 can (16 ounces) sauerkraut, undrained
1 cup applesauce
1 small onion, finely chopped
2 tablespoons packed brown sugar
¼ teaspoon caraway seed
¼ teaspoon garlic powder

Arrange ribs in oblong baking dish, 12 x 7½ x 2 inches, with larger pieces toward sides of dish. Cover loosely and microwave until meat is no longer pink, 13 to 15 minutes; drain. Turn and rearrange ribs.

Mix remaining ingredients; spoon onto ribs. Cover loosely and microwave until sauerkraut mixture is hot and ribs are done, 10 to 12 minutes.

4 or 5 servings.

BARBECUED RIBS AND PEACHES

2½ to 3 pounds fresh pork country-style ribs, cut into serving pieces
1 teaspoon salt
⅛ teaspoon pepper
1 can (16 ounces) sliced peaches
2 teaspoons cornstarch
¼ cup chili sauce
  Dash of garlic powder

Sprinkle pork ribs with salt and pepper. Place in 2 layers in square baking dish, 8 x 8 x 2 inches. Cover loosely and microwave 6 minutes; rearrange ribs. Cover loosely and microwave until ribs are no longer pink, 7 to 8 minutes; drain.

Drain peaches, reserving ⅓ cup syrup. Mix reserved peach syrup, the cornstarch, chili sauce and garlic powder; spoon over ribs. Cover loosely and microwave until ribs are tender, 10 to 12 minutes, basting with sauce every 4 minutes. Spoon peaches around ribs. Cover loosely and microwave until hot, 1 to 2 minutes.

5 or 6 servings.

GLAZED HAM PATTIES

1 pound ground fully cooked ham (about 3 cups)
1 egg
¼ cup dry bread crumbs
1 tablespoon finely chopped onion
2 tablespoons milk
2 teaspoons dried parsley flakes
1 teaspoon prepared mustard
2 tablespoons packed brown sugar
2 tablespoons honey
1 teaspoon vinegar
⅛ teaspoon ground cloves
1 tablespoon orange juice

Mix ham, egg, bread crumbs, onion, milk, parsley flakes and mustard. Shape into 4 patties about 3½ inches in diameter. Place in square baking dish, 8 x 8 x 2 inches.

Mix brown sugar, honey, vinegar and cloves; spread half of the mixture over patties. Stir orange juice into remaining mixture; reserve.

Cover patties loosely and microwave 4 minutes; turn dish one-quarter turn. Microwave until patties are firm in center, 3 to 4 minutes. Serve reserved glaze over patties.

4 servings.

BOLOGNA ROMANOFF

- 1 package (5.5 ounces) noodles Romanoff
- 2 cups water
- 2 tablespoons margarine or butter
- 2 teaspoons instant minced onion
- ¼ teaspoon salt
- 1 package (10 ounces) frozen peas
- 1 package (16 ounces) ring bologna, cut into 1-inch pieces
  Parmesan cheese (optional)

Mix noodles, Sauce Mix, water, margarine, onion and salt in 2-quart casserole. Cover and microwave 5 minutes; stir. Cover and microwave until noodles are tender, 2 to 3 minutes.

Stir in peas and bologna. Cover and microwave 3 minutes; stir. Cover and microwave until peas are tender, 2 to 3 minutes. Sprinkle with Parmesan cheese.

4 or 5 servings.

MICROWAVE TIP

Special meat thermometers that can be used in the oven during microwaving are available. However, regular mercury-type thermometers should not be used during microwaving. If it is necessary to check the internal temperature of a food with this type thermometer, first remove the food from the oven and then check the temperature. Be sure to remove the thermometer if additional microwaving is necessary.

HERB-GLAZED LAMB CHOPS

- 2 or 3 lamb shoulder or leg chops (¾ to 1 pound), about ½ inch thick
- ½ cup water
- 1 tablespoon cornstarch
- 1 teaspoon soy sauce
- ½ teaspoon sugar
- ¼ teaspoon salt
- ¼ teaspoon dried basil leaves
- ⅛ teaspoon dry mustard

Cover and microwave lamb chops in square baking dish, 8 x 8 x 2 inches, 3 minutes; turn. Cover and microwave until no longer pink, 2 to 2½ minutes. Mix remaining ingredients; pour over chops. Cover and microwave 5 minutes. Let stand 5 minutes; turn and rearrange chops. Cover and microwave until tender, 5 to 8 minutes.

2 or 3 servings.

MINTED LAMB MEATBALLS

- 1 pound ground lamb
- 1 egg
- ¼ cup dry bread crumbs
- ¼ cup milk
- 2 tablespoons finely chopped onion
- ½ teaspoon salt
- ¼ teaspoon paprika
- ⅛ teaspoon pepper
- ¼ cup mint-flavored apple jelly
- ¼ teaspoon dried tarragon leaves

Mix all ingredients except jelly and tarragon. Shape into 12 meatballs, about 1¾ inches in diameter. Place in oblong baking dish, 10 x 6 x 1½ inches. Cover loosely and microwave until done, 1 to 2 minutes; drain.

Mix jelly and tarragon; spoon over meatballs. Cover loosely and microwave until jelly is melted, 1 to 2 minutes. Stir to coat meatballs evenly.

4 or 5 servings.

CHICKEN 'N DRESSING

2½ - pound broiler-fryer chicken
1 package (6 ounces) chicken-flavored stuffing mix
1¼ cups water
    Paprika

Cut chicken into pieces; cut each breast half into halves. Mix stuffing mix (with seasoning packet) and water in oblong baking dish, 12 x 7½ x 2 inches. Arrange chicken skin sides up and thickest parts to outside on stuffing. Sprinkle with paprika. Cover loosely and microwave until chicken is done, 20 to 25 minutes.

8 servings.

ORANGE-GLAZED CHICKEN

2½ - pound broiler-fryer chicken, cut up
½ cup orange marmalade
¼ cup orange juice
2 tablespoons cornstarch
2 tablespoons packed brown sugar
2 tablespoons lemon juice
1½ teaspoons salt
½ orange, sliced and quartered

Arrange chicken pieces skin sides up and thickest parts to outside in oblong baking dish, 12 x 7½ x 2 inches. Cover loosely and microwave 15 minutes.

Mix marmalade, orange juice, cornstarch, brown sugar, lemon juice and salt in 4-cup glass measure. Spoon in juices from chicken. Microwave sauce 2½ minutes; stir. Microwave to boiling, 1 to 1½ minutes. Boil until sauce is thickened and translucent, 1 minute longer. Stir in orange slices.

Spoon sauce over chicken. Cover loosely and microwave until chicken is done, 10 to 15 minutes. If desired, garnish with parsley.

6 servings.

BARBECUED CHICKEN

2½ - pound broiler-fryer chicken
1 cup catsup
½ cup water
¼ cup Worcestershire sauce
¼ cup vinegar
¼ cup packed brown sugar
1 medium onion, chopped
2 tablespoons cornstarch
1 tablespoon lemon juice
1 teaspoon salt
1 teaspoon celery seed
¼ teaspoon liquid smoke
2 dashes Tabasco sauce

Cut chicken into pieces; cut each breast half into halves. Arrange chicken skin sides up and thickest parts to outside in oblong baking dish, 12 x 7½ x 2 inches. Mix remaining ingredients in 4-cup glass measure. Microwave 3 minutes; stir. Microwave until mixture boils and thickens, 2 to 3 minutes. Pour sauce over chicken.

Cover loosely and microwave 10 minutes. Rearrange chicken and baste with sauce. Cover loosely and microwave until chicken is done, 10 to 15 minutes, basting with sauce every 5 minutes.

8 servings.

MICROWAVE TIP

To ensure even cooking in the microwave oven, arrange chicken in the baking dish with the larger, meatier portions and pieces toward the edge of the dish and the smaller, less meaty pieces toward the center of the dish.

CHICKEN WITH SAUCE SUPREME

2½ - pound broiler-fryer chicken
  1 teaspoon salt
  ⅛ teaspoon pepper
  1 can (10¾ ounces) condensed cream of chicken soup
  2 teaspoons dried parsley flakes
  1 can (16 ounces) whole onions, drained
  3 cups hot cooked rice

Cut chicken into pieces; cut each breast half into halves. Arrange chicken skin sides up and thickest parts to outside in oblong baking dish, 12 x 7½ x 2 inches. Sprinkle with salt and pepper. Cover loosely and microwave until chicken is done, 20 to 25 minutes.

Remove chicken from dish; reserve juices. Stir soup and parsley into chicken juices. Arrange chicken in dish, coating with soup mixture. Add onions. Cover loosely and microwave until hot, 7 to 9 minutes. Serve with rice.

8 servings.

GOLDEN PARSLEYED CHICKEN

2½ - pound broiler-fryer chicken
  1 egg
  1 tablespoon water
 30 round buttery crackers, finely crushed (about 1⅓ cups)
  2 tablespoons dried parsley flakes
  ½ teaspoon salt
  ⅛ teaspoon pepper

Cut chicken into pieces; cut each breast half into halves. Beat egg and water. Mix cracker crumbs, parsley, salt and pepper. Dip chicken pieces into egg mixture, then coat with crumbs. Arrange chicken skin sides up and thickest parts to outside in oblong baking dish, 12 x 7½ x 2 inches. Cover loosely and microwave until done, 20 to 25 minutes.

8 servings.

CHICKEN ALMONDINE

1½ cups water
  ½ package (10-ounce size) frozen peas (1 cup)
  1 package (6 ounces) noodles almondine
  1 to 1½ pounds chicken pieces
    Paprika

Microwave water and peas in 4-cup glass measure to boiling, 5½ to 6½ minutes.

Place noodles and Seasoned Sauce Mix in square baking dish, 8 x 8 x 2 inches. Stir in hot water and peas. Arrange chicken pieces on top, skin sides up and thickest parts to outside, turning to coat with sauce. Sprinkle with paprika. Cover loosely and microwave until chicken is done and noodles are tender, 12 to 15 minutes. Sprinkle with almonds.

4 servings.

CHICKEN CURRY CASSEROLE

  2 packages (10 ounces each) frozen cut asparagus
  1 can (10¾ ounces) condensed cream of chicken soup
  ⅓ cup mayonnaise or salad dressing
  ⅓ cup milk
  1 tablespoon chopped pimiento
1¼ teaspoons salt
  ½ teaspoon curry powder
  ⅛ teaspoon pepper
  3 cups cut-up cooked chicken
  ⅓ cup dry bread crumbs

Microwave frozen asparagus in packages on paper towel until almost tender, 7 to 8 minutes; drain. Arrange in oblong baking dish, 12 x 7½ x 2 inches.

Mix soup, mayonnaise, milk, pimiento, salt, curry powder and pepper; stir in chicken. Spoon onto asparagus. Sprinkle with bread crumbs. Cover loosely and microwave until hot, 8 to 10 minutes.

6 servings.

FRIED CHICKEN TERIYAKI

1 package (2 pounds) frozen fried chicken
½ cup soy sauce
3 tablespoons honey
1 tablespoon vinegar
1 tablespoon dry white wine
¼ teaspoon ground ginger
⅛ teaspoon garlic powder
2 tablespoons chopped green onions
1 can (11 ounces) mandarin oranges, drained (reserve syrup)
2 tablespoons cornstarch
½ cup water

Arrange frozen chicken with thickest parts to outside in oblong baking dish, 12 x 7½ x 2 inches. Mix soy sauce, honey, vinegar, wine, ginger and garlic powder in 4-cup glass measure. Brush chicken with some soy mixture; reserve remaining mixture. Sprinkle green onions over chicken. Cover loosely and microwave until chicken is hot, 15 to 18 minutes.

Stir reserved mandarin orange syrup, the cornstarch and water into reserved soy mixture. Microwave 2 minutes; stir. Microwave until mixture boils and thickens, 2 to 3 minutes. Stir in orange segments. Serve sauce over chicken.

6 servings.

CHICKEN BREASTS DIVAN

6 small chicken breast halves (about 2 pounds)
2 packages (8 ounces each) frozen broccoli spears
1 can (10¾ ounces) condensed cream of chicken soup
¾ cup mayonnaise or salad dressing
½ teaspoon curry powder
1 tablespoon margarine or butter
⅓ cup dry bread crumbs

Arrange chicken breasts skin sides up in oblong baking dish, 12 x 7½ x 2 inches. Cover loosely and microwave until chicken is done, 15 to 17 minutes. Drain and reserve juices.

Microwave frozen broccoli in package on paper towel until tender, 8 to 10 minutes; drain. Arrange broccoli spears under chicken breasts. Mix soup, mayonnaise, curry powder and ½ cup reserved juices from chicken; pour over chicken.

Microwave margarine uncovered in small dish until melted, 30 to 45 seconds. Stir in bread crumbs. Sprinkle over chicken. Cover loosely and microwave until hot, 7 to 9 minutes.

6 servings.

MICROWAVE TIPS

To thaw a frozen boneless turkey roast in the microwave oven, allow 3 minutes per pound microwave time at a high setting with 5-minute standing times after every 2 minutes of microwave time. If your oven has a defrost setting, follow manufacturer's instructions for timing.

All food that is not going to be cooked or served immediately should be refrigerated until that time.

BERRIED TURKEY ROAST

2 - pound frozen boneless turkey roast
½ can whole cranberry sauce (about 1 cup)
1 tablespoon orange juice
2 tablespoons honey

Thaw turkey roast completely. Place top side down in loaf dish, 9 x 5 x 3 inches. Cover loosely and microwave 10 minutes. Turn top side up. Cover loosely and microwave 5 minutes.

Cut turkey into 10 slices, cutting to within ½ inch of bottom. Combine cranberry sauce, orange juice and honey; spoon over turkey. Microwave uncovered until turkey is done (170°), 5 to 7 minutes.

10 servings.

TURKEY AND HAM ROULADEN

18 spears fresh asparagus (about 1 pound)
2 tablespoons water
6 thin slices cooked turkey (about 6 ounces)
6 thin slices cooked ham (about 6 ounces)
1 can (10¾ ounces) condensed cream of mushroom soup
¼ cup milk
¼ cup grated Parmesan cheese

Break off tough ends of asparagus at point where stalks snap easily. Place asparagus in 2-quart casserole. Add water. Cover and microwave until tender, 7 to 8 minutes; drain.

Wrap each turkey and ham slice around 3 asparagus spears. Place in oblong baking dish, 12 x 7½ x 2 inches. Mix soup, milk and cheese; pour over rolls. Cover loosely and microwave until hot, 8 to 10 minutes.

6 servings.

TURKEY AND WILD RICE CASSEROLE

1 can (4 ounces) mushroom stems and pieces
3 tablespoons flour
1⅓ cups water
1½ teaspoons instant beef bouillon
½ teaspoon salt
1 package (6 ounces) long-grain and wild rice mix
2 packages (8 ounces each) frozen broccoli spears
2 cups cut-up cooked turkey

Mix mushrooms (with liquid) and flour in 4-cup glass measure. Stir in water, bouillon and salt. Microwave 3 minutes; stir. Microwave until mixture boils and thickens, 2 to 3 minutes, stirring every minute.

Pour rice (with seasoning packet) into oblong baking dish, 12 x 7½ x 2 inches. Add water and butter as directed on package. Cover and microwave 10 minutes. Let stand 5 minutes; stir. Cover and microwave until rice is tender, 7 to 9 minutes.

Microwave frozen broccoli in packages on paper towel until tender, 10 to 12 minutes; drain.

Top rice with broccoli, turkey and mushroom sauce. Cover loosely and microwave until hot, 6 to 8 minutes.

6 servings.

TOMATO AND CHEESE FILLETS

1 tablespoon margarine or butter
½ pound fish fillets
¼ teaspoon salt
  Dash of pepper
2 teaspoons finely chopped onion
1 medium tomato, chopped
¼ cup shredded Cheddar cheese (about
  1 ounce)

Microwave margarine uncovered in square baking dish, 8 x 8 x 2 inches. Place fish fillets in
dish, turning to coat with margarine. Sprinkle
with salt and pepper; top with onion, tomato and
cheese. Cover tightly and microwave until fish
flakes easily with fork, 2½ to 3 minutes.

2 or 3 servings.

POACHED FISH

1 pound fish fillets
2 teaspoons instant chicken bouillon
½ cup water
¼ teaspoon salt
¼ teaspoon dried parsley flakes
¼ teaspoon chopped chives
1 tablespoon lemon juice
4 peppercorns
1 small bay leaf
6 lemon slices

If fillets are large, cut into serving pieces. Place
in square baking dish, 8 x 8 x 2 inches. Sprinkle
with instant bouillon.

Mix water, salt, parsley, chives, lemon juice,
peppercorns and bay leaf; pour over fish. Top
with lemon slices. Cover tightly and microwave
until fish flakes easily with fork, 4½ to 5 minutes. Remove fish from broth with slotted
spoon.

5 or 6 servings.

TARTAR-SAUCED FILLETS

1 tablespoon margarine or butter
1 tablespoon flour
1 teaspoon instant chicken bouillon
⅛ teaspoon salt
½ cup water
¼ cup mayonnaise or salad dressing
1 tablespoon sweet pickle relish
1 teaspoon finely chopped onion
1 teaspoon lemon juice
1 package (14 ounces) frozen fried fish fillets

Microwave margarine in 2-cup glass measure
until melted, 30 seconds to 1 minute. Stir in
flour, bouillon, salt and water. Microwave 1
minute; stir. Microwave until sauce boils and
thickens, 30 seconds to 1 minute. Stir in
mayonnaise, relish, onion and lemon juice.

Arrange fillets in square baking dish, 8 x 8 x 2
inches. Cover loosely and microwave 5 minutes; turn dish one-quarter turn. Microwave until
fish is hot, 3 to 4 minutes. Spoon sauce onto
fish. Microwave uncovered until hot, 1 to 2
minutes.

4 servings.

DILLED FISH

2 tablespoons margarine or butter
½ pound fish fillets
¼ teaspoon dill weed
  Salt
  Pepper
  Lemon slices

Microwave margarine uncovered in square baking dish, 8 x 8 x 2 inches, until melted, 30
seconds to 1 minute. Place fillets in dish, turning to coat with margarine. Sprinkle with dill
weed, salt and pepper. Cover tightly and
microwave until fish flakes easily with fork, 2 to
2½ minutes. Garnish with lemon slices.

2 or 3 servings.

STUFFED SOLE RINGS

1   package (10 ounces) frozen chopped
    broccoli
¼   cup mayonnaise or salad dressing
¼   cup chopped almonds or pecans
1   tablespoon lemon juice
¼   teaspoon salt
1   pound sole fillets
¼   teaspoon salt
⅛   teaspoon pepper

Microwave frozen broccoli in package on paper towel until thawed, 4 to 5 minutes; drain. Mix with mayonnaise, almonds, lemon juice and ¼ teaspoon salt.

Sprinkle fillets with ¼ teaspoon salt and the pepper. Cut fillets lengthwise into strips 1½ to 2 inches wide. Bring ends of each strip together, forming a circle about 2 inches in diameter; fasten ends with wooden pick. Arrange in square baking dish, 8 x 8 x 2 inches. Spoon broccoli mixture into center of each circle. Cover tightly and microwave until fish flakes easily with fork, 5 to 6½ minutes.

5 or 6 servings.

HOT TUNA SALAD

1   package (10 ounces) frozen peas
1   can (6½ ounces) tuna, drained
½   cup mayonnaise or salad dressing
1   tablespoon sweet pickle relish
1   can (1½ ounces) shoestring potatoes

Cover and microwave peas in 1½-quart casserole until hot, 3½ to 4 minutes.

Stir in tuna, mayonnaise, relish and 1 cup of the potatoes. Cover and microwave until hot, 3½ to 4 minutes. Sprinkle with remaining potatoes.

3 or 4 servings.

TUNA-MACARONI BAKE

1   package (7.25 ounces) macaroni
      and cheese
1½   cups water
1   can (10¾ ounces) condensed cream of
      mushroom soup
1   can (6½ ounces) tuna, drained
2   tablespoons margarine or butter

Cover and microwave macaroni, Sauce Mix and water in 1½-quart casserole 4 minutes; stir. Cover and microwave 3 minutes.

Stir in soup, tuna and margarine. Cover and microwave until macaroni is tender, 5 to 6 minutes.

6 servings.

SEAFOOD NEWBURG

1   can (10¾ ounces) condensed cream of
    shrimp soup
¼   cup milk
1   tablespoon chopped chives
2   tablespoons dry white wine (optional)
    Dash of garlic powder
1   package (6 ounces) frozen cooked
    crabmeat and shrimp
4   slices toast or 2 cups hot cooked rice

Mix all ingredients except toast in 1-quart casserole. Cover and microwave until hot and seafood is done, 7 to 8 minutes, stirring every 2 minutes. Serve over toast.

4 servings.

SALMON-RICE BAKE

1½ cups instant rice
1½ cups water
 1 can (10¾ ounces) condensed cream of
     mushroom soup
 1 can (7¾ ounces) salmon, drained
     and flaked
 2 tablespoons margarine or butter
 1 tablespoon dried parsley flakes
 ½ teaspoon salt

Mix all ingredients in 1½-quart casserole. Cover and microwave 5 minutes; stir. Cover and microwave until rice is tender, 6 to 7 minutes. Stir before serving.

3 or 4 servings.

SEAFOOD CREPES

 1 package (10 ounces) frozen chopped
     spinach
 ⅓ cup margarine or butter
 ¼ cup all-purpose flour
 1 can (13¾ ounces) chicken broth
     (1¾ cups)
 ½ teaspoon salt
     Dash of pepper
 1 tablespoon lemon juice
 1 can (6½ ounces) tuna, drained
 1 can (4½ ounces) medium shrimp, drained
 1 cup shredded Swiss cheese (about
     4 ounces)
12 crepes (8 to 10 inches in diameter)
     Dried parsley flakes

Microwave frozen spinach in package on paper towel until thawed, 4 to 5 minutes; drain.

Microwave margarine in 4-cup glass measure until melted, 30 seconds to 1 minute. Stir in flour, broth, salt and pepper. Microwave 2 minutes; stir. Microwave until mixture boils and thickens, 1½ to 2 minutes, stirring every minute. Stir in lemon juice.

Mix spinach, tuna, shrimp, cheese and ¾ cup of the sauce. Place slightly rounded ¼ cup seafood mixture in center of each crepe. Roll up crepes; place seam side down in row in oblong baking dish, 12 x 7½ x 2 inches. Pour remaining sauce over rolls; sprinkle with parsley. Cover loosely and microwave until hot, 6 to 7 minutes.

6 servings.

INDIVIDUAL SALMON LOAVES

 1 can (16 ounces) salmon, drained and flaked
 2 eggs, beaten
 ⅓ cup dry bread crumbs
 2 tablespoons milk
 ½ teaspoon grated lemon peel
 ½ teaspoon chopped chives
 ½ teaspoon salt
     Creamed Peas (below)

Mix all ingredients except Creamed Peas. Press into 6 six-ounce custard cups. Arrange in circle in microwave oven. Microwave 3 minutes; rearrange cups. Microwave until set, 1½ to 2½ minutes.

Prepare Creamed Peas. Invert salmon loaves on serving plate; serve with peas.

6 servings.

CREAMED PEAS

 1 tablespoon margarine or butter
 1 tablespoon flour
 ½ teaspoon salt
     Dash of pepper
 ⅔ cup milk
 1 can (8 ounces) peas, drained

Microwave margarine in 2-cup glass measure until melted, 30 seconds to 1 minute. Blend in flour, salt and pepper; stir in milk. Microwave 1 minute. Stir in peas. Microwave until mixture boils and thickens, 1 to 2 minutes.

EGGS IN TOAST CUPS

2 slices bread
2 tablespoons margarine or butter, softened
2 eggs
Salt
Pepper

Flatten bread slices with rolling pin to ¼-inch thickness. Spread 1 side of each slice with margarine. Press each slice buttered side down into 6-ounce custard cup. Microwave uncovered 1 minute; rearrange cups. Microwave until crisp, 1 to 1½ minutes.

Break an egg into each cup. Microwave uncovered until eggs are set, 1 to 1½ minutes. Sprinkle with salt and pepper.

2 servings.

MEXICAN-STYLE EGG CUPS

4 eggs
¼ cup milk
¼ teaspoon salt
Dash of pepper
2 tablespoons chopped green chilies
4 flour tortillas (6 inches in diameter)
1 medium tomato, chopped
½ cup shredded Monterey Jack or Colby cheese (about 2 ounces)
Taco sauce (optional)

Beat eggs, milk, salt and pepper in 1-quart casserole. Cover and microwave 2 minutes; stir. Cover and microwave until set but still moist, 1 to 1½ minutes. Stir in chilies, breaking up eggs.

Line 4 custard or coffee cups with tortillas. Divide egg mixture among cups; top with tomato and cheese. Microwave until cheese is melted, 1½ to 2½ minutes. Serve with taco sauce.

4 servings.

SCRAMBLED EGGS BENEDICT

1 package (1¼ ounces) Hollandaise sauce mix
4 to 8 thin slices Canadian-style bacon or smoked ham
4 eggs
¼ cup milk
2 tablespoons chopped green pepper (optional)
⅛ teaspoon salt
Dash of pepper
2 English muffins, split and toasted

Mix sauce as directed on package in 2-cup glass measure. Microwave 1 minute; stir. Microwave until mixture boils and thickens, 1 to 1½ minutes, stirring every 30 seconds.

Cover and microwave bacon until hot, 1½ to 2 minutes.

Beat eggs in 1-quart casserole. Beat in milk, green pepper, salt and pepper. Cover and microwave 2 minutes; stir. Cover and microwave until eggs are set but still moist, 1 to 1½ minutes.

Place muffins cut sides up on serving plate. Top each with bacon slice and large spoonful of eggs; spoon sauce over eggs. Microwave uncovered until hot, 1 to 1½ minutes.

4 servings.

CREAMED EGGS ON TOAST

    3 tablespoons margarine or butter
    3 tablespoons flour
    ½ teaspoon dry mustard
    ¼ teaspoon salt
       Dash of pepper
 1 ½ cups milk
    4 hard-cooked eggs, each cut into eighths
    1 teaspoon dried parsley flakes
    4 slices buttered toast

Microwave margarine uncovered in 1-quart casserole until melted, 30 seconds to 1 minute. Blend in flour, mustard, salt and pepper. Stir in milk. Microwave uncovered 2 minutes; stir. Microwave uncovered until mixture boils and thickens, 2 to 3 minutes, stirring every minute. Gently stir in eggs and parsley. Serve over toast.

4 servings.

EASY OMELET

    3 eggs
    3 tablespoons milk
    ¼ cup shredded cheese (about 1 ounce),
       chopped cooked ham or canned sliced
       mushrooms
       Salt
       Pepper

Butter 9-inch pie plate. Beat eggs and milk in pie plate. Microwave uncovered until edge is set, 1 ¼ to 1 ¾ minutes.

Push cooked egg to center; microwave uncovered until edge is set, 1 minute. Sprinkle top with cheese. Microwave uncovered until remaining egg is set but still moist, 30 seconds to 1 minute. Fold omelet in half; slip onto serving plate. Sprinkle with salt and pepper.

1 or 2 servings.

DEVILED EGGS AND NOODLES

       Deviled Eggs (below)
    2 tablespoons chopped onion
    1 tablespoon margarine or butter
 2 ½ cups noodles, cooked
    1 cup dairy sour cream
    ⅓ cup grated Parmesan cheese
    ⅓ cup milk
    ⅓ cup sliced ripe olives
    2 teaspoons poppy seed
    ½ teaspoon salt

Prepare Deviled Eggs. Cover and microwave onion and margarine in 1 ½-quart casserole until onion is tender, 1 ½ to 2 minutes. Stir in remaining ingredients. Cover and microwave until hot, 5 to 6 minutes; stir.

Arrange eggs on noodles. Cover and microwave until eggs are hot, 1 to 2 minutes.

4 servings.

DEVILED EGGS

    3 hard-cooked eggs
    2 tablespoons mayonnaise or salad dressing
    ½ teaspoon prepared mustard
    ⅛ teaspoon salt
       Dash of pepper

Cut eggs lengthwise into halves. Slip out yolks; mash with fork. Mix in remaining ingredients. Fill whites with yolk mixture, heaping it up lightly.

EGGS FLORENTINE

- 2 packages (10 ounces each) frozen chopped spinach
- 2 tablespoons margarine or butter
- 2 tablespoons flour
- ½ teaspoon salt
- ½ teaspoon instant minced onion
- ¼ teaspoon dry mustard
  Dash of pepper
- 1 cup milk
- ⅓ cup shredded Cheddar cheese (about 1½ ounces)
- 1 tablespoon lemon juice
- 6 eggs
  Salt
  Pepper
- 1 tablespoon margarine or butter
- ¼ cup dry bread crumbs

Microwave frozen spinach in packages on paper towel until thawed, 7 to 8 minutes; drain.

Microwave 2 tablespoons margarine in 2-cup glass measure until melted, 30 seconds to 1 minute. Blend in flour, salt, the onion, mustard and dash of pepper. Stir in milk. Microwave 1½ minutes; stir. Microwave until mixture boils and thickens, 2 to 2½ minutes, stirring every minute. Stir in cheese and lemon juice.

Mix spinach and half of the cheese sauce in square baking dish, 8 x 8 x 2 inches; spread evenly in dish. Make 6 indentations in spinach; break an egg into each. Sprinkle with salt and pepper. Pour remaining sauce around eggs. Cover loosely and microwave 6 minutes; turn dish one-quarter turn. Microwave until eggs are done, 3 to 4 minutes.

Microwave 1 tablespoon margarine uncovered until melted, 30 seconds to 1 minute. Stir in bread crumbs; sprinkle over eggs.

6 servings.

EGG FOO YONG CASSEROLE

  Sauce (below)
- ¼ cup chopped onion
- ½ cup chopped celery
- ½ cup chopped green pepper
- 1 tablespoon margarine or butter
- 1 can (16 ounces) bean sprouts, drained
- ⅓ cup sliced water chestnuts
- 1 tablespoon chopped pimiento
- ¾ teaspoon salt
- 6 eggs, beaten

Prepare Sauce. Cover and microwave onion, celery, green pepper and margarine in 1½-quart casserole 2½ minutes; stir. Cover and microwave until vegetables are almost tender, 2 to 2½ minutes.

Stir in remaining ingredients. Cover and microwave until eggs are set but still moist, 5 to 6 minutes, stirring every 2 minutes. Spoon Sauce over each serving.

5 or 6 servings.

SAUCE

- ⅔ cup water
- 1 tablespoon cornstarch
- 1 tablespoon soy sauce
- 1 teaspoon sugar
- 1½ teaspoons vinegar

Mix all ingredients in 2-cup glass measure. Microwave 1 minute; stir. Microwave until mixture boils and thickens, 1 to 1½ minutes, stirring every minute.

SPECIAL MACARONI AND CHEESE

4 slices bacon
2 cups macaroni, cooked
2 cups ½-inch cubes process American
   cheese (about 10 ounces)
¼ cup milk
¼ teaspoon salt
   Dash of pepper

Microwave bacon between paper towels in 1½-quart casserole until crisp, 3 to 4 minutes. Remove bacon and paper towels; reserve bacon.

Pour off all but 1 tablespoon bacon drippings. Add remaining ingredients to drippings. Cover and microwave 3 minutes; stir. Cover and microwave until hot, 3 to 4 minutes. Crumble bacon and sprinkle over top.

4 to 6 servings.

BACON AND MUSHROOM QUICHE

  9-inch Microwaved Pie Shell (page 50)
10 slices bacon
1½ cups shredded Swiss cheese (about
    6 ounces)
  1 can (4 ounces) mushroom stems and
    pieces, drained
1¼ cups half-and-half or evaporated milk
 ¼ teaspoon salt
    Dash of pepper
  3 eggs, beaten
  1 tablespoon chopped chives

Prepare and microwave pie shell. Layer ⅓ of the bacon between paper towels in baking dish. Repeat 2 times. Microwave until crisp, 7 to 9 minutes; cool slightly. Crumble bacon into pie shell. Top with cheese and mushrooms.

Microwave half-and-half in 4-cup glass measure until hot, 2 to 2½ minutes. Beat in salt, pepper and eggs; pour over cheese in pie shell. Sprinkle with chives. Microwave uncovered 4 minutes; turn pie plate one-quarter turn. Microwave until center is just about set, 4½ to 5½ minutes. Let stand a few minutes before cutting.

6 servings.

CHEESY NOODLE BAKE

  1 small onion, chopped
  1 tablespoon margarine or butter
  1 tablespoon flour
 ½ teaspoon dry mustard
 ½ teaspoon salt
    Dash of pepper
 ⅓ cup milk
1½ cups (12 ounces) small-curd cottage
    cheese
  3 cups noodles, cooked
  1 teaspoon dried parsley flakes
 ¾ cup shredded Cheddar cheese (about
    3 ounces)

Cover and microwave onion and margarine in 1½-quart casserole until onion is tender, 2 to 3 minutes.

Blend in flour, mustard, salt and pepper. Stir in milk. Microwave uncovered 1½ minutes; stir. Microwave uncovered until mixture boils and thickens, 30 seconds to 1 minute.

Stir in cottage cheese, noodles and parsley. Cover and microwave until hot, 5 to 6 minutes; stir. Sprinkle with cheese. Microwave uncovered until cheese is melted, 2 to 2½ minutes.

4 or 5 servings.

VEGETABLES AND BREADS

ASPARAGUS-ALMOND SAUTE

¼ cup sliced or slivered almonds
2 tablespoons margarine or butter
3 cups 1-inch pieces asparagus
  (about 1¼ pounds)*
1 cup sliced mushrooms*
1 small clove garlic, minced
½ teaspoon seasoned salt

Combine almonds and margarine in 1-quart casserole. Microwave uncovered until almonds are toasted, 4 to 5 minutes, stirring every minute. Remove almonds with slotted spoon; reserve.

Add asparagus, mushrooms and garlic to drippings in casserole. Cover and microwave until asparagus is tender, 8 to 9 minutes. Stir in salt; sprinkle with reserved almonds.

4 or 5 servings.

*1 package (10 ounces) frozen asparagus, broken apart, and 1 can (4 ounces) mushroom stems and pieces, drained, can be substituted for the fresh asparagus and mushrooms.

SWEET-AND-SOUR BEANS

2 slices bacon
1 small onion, sliced
¼ cup sugar
1 tablespoon flour
  Dash of pepper
⅓ cup vinegar
1 can (16 ounces) cut green beans, drained
1 can (16 ounces) wax beans, drained

Place bacon in 1½-quart casserole. Cover with paper towel and microwave until crisp, 2 to 3 minutes. Remove bacon and drain on paper towel.

Add onion to bacon fat in casserole. Cover and microwave until onion is crisp-tender, 2 to 3 minutes.

Stir in sugar, flour, pepper and vinegar. Cover and microwave to boiling, 1½ to 2 minutes.

Stir in beans. Cover and microwave until hot, 3 to 3½ minutes. Crumble bacon; sprinkle over top.

5 servings.

BEAN AND ONION BAKE

1 package (10 ounces) frozen French-style green beans
1 package (10 ounces) frozen onions in cheese sauce
½ to 1 can (8½-ounce size) water chestnuts, drained and sliced
¼ teaspoon salt

Microwave frozen green beans in package on paper towel until tender, 8 to 9 minutes; drain.

Cut small slit in onion pouch; microwave onions until hot, 6 to 7 minutes.

Mix green beans, onions, water chestnuts and salt. Cover and microwave until hot, 2 to 3 minutes.

5 servings.

PICKLED BEETS

1 can (16 ounces) sliced beets
¼ cup sugar
¼ cup vinegar
4 whole cloves

Drain beets, reserving ¼ cup liquid. Mix reserved beet liquid, the sugar, vinegar and cloves in 1-quart casserole or bowl. Cover and microwave to boiling, 1½ to 2½ minutes. Stir in beets. Cover and refrigerate at least 4 hours.

6 servings.

BUTTERED BROCCOLI

2 packages (10 ounces each) frozen broccoli spears
1 clove garlic, minced
¼ teaspoon dried rosemary leaves
¼ teaspoon salt
2 tablespoons margarine or butter
¼ cup crushed salad croutons (optional)

Microwave frozen broccoli in packages on paper towel until almost tender, 10 to 12 minutes; drain. Place broccoli in 1½-quart casserole or serving dish.

Sprinkle broccoli with garlic, rosemary and salt; dot with margarine. Cover and microwave until margarine melts, 1 to 2 minutes. Toss lightly; sprinkle with croutons.

5 or 6 servings.

BROCCOLI ITALIANO

1 pound broccoli
2 tablespoons water
2 tablespoons vegetable oil
1 clove garlic, minced
1 tablespoon vinegar
½ teaspoon salt
¼ teaspoon Italian seasoning
1 tablespoon margarine or butter
2 tablespoons dry bread crumbs
2 tablespoons grated Parmesan cheese

Arrange broccoli stem ends to outside in dish. Add water. Cover and microwave until broccoli is tender, 8 to 10 minutes; drain. Mix oil, garlic, vinegar, salt and Italian seasoning; pour over broccoli.

Microwave margarine uncovered in small dish until melted, 30 seconds to 1 minute. Stir in bread crumbs and cheese. Sprinkle over broccoli. Microwave uncovered until hot, 1 to 2 minutes.

5 or 6 servings.

BROCCOLI, CHEESE AND TOMATO BAKE

2 packages (10 ounces each) frozen broccoli spears
1 package (1.5 ounces) cheese sauce mix
2 medium tomatoes, sliced
½ cup croutons, crushed

Microwave frozen broccoli in packages on paper towel until almost tender, 10 to 12 minutes; drain. Place broccoli in 1½-quart serving dish.

Prepare cheese sauce mix as directed on package in 2-cup glass measure. Microwave 1½ minutes; stir. Microwave to boiling, 1½ to 2 minutes.

Arrange tomato slices on broccoli. Top with cheese sauce; sprinkle with croutons. Microwave uncovered until hot, 2 to 3 minutes.

8 servings.

MICROWAVE TIPS

Frozen vegetables are often microwaved right in the paper freezer container. Because the printed waxed paper covering can mark the oven floor, you may wish to remove this covering or place the package on a paper towel.

You can also microwave frozen vegetables in plastic pouches and/or boil-in bags. Be sure to make a slit in the pouch or bag to allow excess steam to escape. Pouches and boil-in bags can be placed directly on the oven floor.

BUTTERED CABBAGE WEDGES

½ medium head cabbage, cut into 4 to 6 wedges
2 tablespoons water
½ teaspoon caraway seed
2 tablespoons margarine or butter
Salt

Arrange cabbage wedges in dish with narrow ends toward center. Add water; sprinkle with caraway seed. Cover and microwave 7 minutes; turn dish one-quarter turn. Microwave until crisp-tender, 5 to 6 minutes; drain.

Microwave margarine uncovered until melted, 30 seconds to 1 minute; drizzle over cabbage. Sprinkle with salt.

4 to 6 servings.

ORANGE-BUTTERED CARROTS

2 cups sliced carrots
2 tablespoons water
2 tablespoons margarine or butter
1 tablespoon sugar
1 teaspoon grated orange peel
¼ teaspoon salt

Cover and microwave carrots and water in 1-quart casserole or bowl 4 minutes. Let stand 5 minutes; stir. Cover and microwave until carrots are tender, 5 to 6 minutes; drain. Stir in remaining ingredients.

3 servings.

CAULIFLOWER WITH CHEESE SAUCE

1 medium head cauliflower (about 1½ pounds)
2 tablespoons water
1 jar (8 ounces) pasteurized process cheese spread
1 tomato, chopped (optional)

Place cauliflower core end down in dish; add water. Cover and microwave until cauliflower is just tender, about 8 minutes; drain.

Remove cover from cheese spread; microwave cheese spread (in jar) until softened, 30 seconds to 1 minute. Pour over cauliflower. Garnish with tomato.

6 servings.

CREAMED CORN

3 slices bacon
2 tablespoons chopped onion
1 tablespoon chopped green pepper
1 tablespoon flour
½ cup dairy sour cream
1 can (16 ounces) whole kernel corn, drained

Place bacon in 1-quart casserole. Cover with paper towel and microwave until crisp, 2½ to 3 minutes. Remove bacon and drain on paper towel.

Add onion and green pepper to bacon fat in casserole. Cover and microwave until vegetables are tender, 2½ to 3 minutes.

Stir in flour, sour cream and corn. Cover and microwave 2 minutes; stir. Cover and microwave until hot, 1 to 2 minutes. Crumble bacon; sprinkle over corn.

5 servings.

BUTTERED CORN ON THE COB

¼ cup margarine or butter
1 tablespoon chopped chives
1 package (4 ears) frozen corn on the cob
Grated Parmesan cheese (optional)

Microwave margarine and chives uncovered in baking dish until margarine is melted, 30 seconds to 1 minute.

Arrange corn in baking dish, turning to coat with margarine. Cover loosely and microwave 6 minutes; turn and rearrange ears. Cover and microwave until corn is done, 5 to 7 minutes. Sprinkle with cheese.

4 servings.

VEGETABLE MEDLEY

1 package (6 ounces) hash brown potatoes with onions
1 can (11 ounces) condensed Cheddar cheese soup
1 can (16 ounces) French-style green beans, drained
1 can (3 ounces) French fried onions
¼ teaspoon salt
⅛ teaspoon pepper
⅛ teaspoon dry mustard

Pour enough boiling water over potatoes to cover in 2-quart casserole or bowl. Let stand 5 minutes; drain thoroughly.

Reserve ½ cup of the onions; stir remaining onions and remaining ingredients into potatoes. Cover and microwave 5 minutes; stir. Top with reserved onions. Cover and microwave until hot and bubbly, 4 to 5 minutes.

8 servings.

MICROWAVE TIPS

You will find that vegetables cook very well in the microwave oven and, because they cook in their own moisture, very little additional liquid is necessary. For fresh vegetables, a few tablespoons of water are added, but for most frozen vegetables, no additional liquid is necessary.

Salt sprinkled over vegetables can toughen the vegetables and may cake. It's best to add salt to the water before adding the vegetables or sprinkle on vegetables after microwaving.

CHEESY HASH BROWNS

- 1 package (6 ounces) hash brown potatoes with onions
- ½ cup chopped green onions
- 1 package (4 ounces) shredded sharp Cheddar cheese
- ½ teaspoon salt
- 3 tablespoons margarine or butter
- ⅓ cup water

Pour enough boiling water over potatoes to cover. Let stand 5 minutes; drain thoroughly.

Layer half each of the potatoes, onions, cheese, salt and margarine in 3-quart casserole. Repeat with other half of the potatoes, onions, salt and margarine; reserve remaining cheese. Pour ⅓ cup water over potato mixture. Cover and microwave 6 to 7 minutes.

Sprinkle with reserved cheese. Cover and microwave 2 minutes. Let stand uncovered 5 minutes before serving.

4 to 6 servings.

EASY AU GRATIN POTATO-TOMATO

- 2½ cups water
- 1 package (5.5 ounces) au gratin potatoes
- ⅔ cup milk
- 2 tablespoons margarine or butter
- 1 can (4 ounces) mushroom stems and pieces, drained
- 1 to 2 medium tomatoes, chopped
- ½ cup croutons, crushed

Cover and microwave water to boiling in 3-quart casserole, 6 to 7 minutes.

Stir in potato slices, Sauce Mix, milk, margarine and mushrooms. Cover and microwave until tender, 15 to 20 minutes. Stir in tomato; top with croutons.

9 servings.

POTATO LOGS

- 1 cup water
- ⅓ cup milk
- ½ teaspoon salt
- 1⅔ cups mashed potato puffs (dry)
- 1 egg, beaten
- 2 tablespoons margarine or butter
- ¼ cup finely chopped onion
- 2 tablespoons grated Parmesan cheese
- 1 teaspoon dried parsley flakes
- ⅓ cup crushed corn flakes

Microwave water, milk and salt to boiling in 4-cup glass measure, 3 to 4 minutes. Stir in potato puffs; beat in egg. Cool about 30 minutes.

Microwave margarine and onion uncovered until onion is tender, 3 to 3½ minutes. Stir into cooled potatoes with cheese and parsley flakes.

Shape ⅓ cup potatoes into log about 5 inches long. Roll in corn flakes. Repeat with remaining potatoes. Cover with paper towel and microwave until hot, 5 to 6 minutes.

6 servings.

HERBED POTATOES

3 or 4 medium potatoes
1 small onion, thinly sliced
2 tablespoons margarine or butter
1 teaspoon dried parsley flakes
½ teaspoon salt
½ teaspoon dried dill weed
¼ teaspoon paprika

Make crosswise cuts ½ inch apart in each potato, not cutting all the way through. Place an onion slice in each cut. Cover and microwave until potatoes are almost tender, 4½ to 5½ minutes.

Microwave margarine uncovered until melted, 30 seconds to 1 minute. Stir in remaining ingredients; drizzle over potatoes. Cover and microwave until potatoes are tender, 4 to 5 minutes.

3 or 4 servings.

TWICE-BAKED POTATOES

4 medium potatoes
1 jar (5 ounces) Neufchâtel cheese spread with pimiento
¼ cup milk
2 tablespoons margarine or butter
½ teaspoon salt
Dash of pepper
Chopped chives

Prick potatoes in several places with fork. Microwave on paper towel 7 minutes; turn over and rearrange potatoes. Microwave until just tender, about 4 minutes. Let stand until cool enough to handle, about 15 minutes.

Cut potatoes lengthwise into halves; scoop out inside, leaving a ¼-inch shell. Mash potatoes until no lumps remain; beat in cheese, milk, margarine, salt and pepper until fluffy. Spoon mixture into potato shells. Sprinkle with chives. Microwave uncovered until hot, 4 to 5 minutes.

8 servings.

GLAZED SWEET POTATOES

1 can (18 ounces) vacuum-pack sweet potatoes
2 tablespoons margarine or butter, cut into pieces
⅓ cup packed brown sugar
⅛ teaspoon ground nutmeg

Gently mix all ingredients. Cover and microwave 3 minutes; stir gently. Cover and microwave until hot, 2 to 3 minutes.

4 servings.

PINEAPPLE-MALLOW SWEET POTATOES

1 can (18 ounces) vacuum-pack sweet potatoes
1 can (8 ounces) crushed pineapple, drained
1 cup miniature marshmallows
¼ cup margarine or butter, softened
1 teaspoon grated orange peel
¼ teaspoon salt
1 tablespoon margarine or butter
¼ cup packed brown sugar
¼ cup chopped pecans or walnuts

Mash potatoes in 1½-quart casserole or bowl. Stir in pineapple, marshmallows, ¼ cup margarine, the orange peel and salt.

Microwave 1 tablespoon margarine uncovered in 10-ounce custard cup until melted, 30 seconds to 1 minute. Stir in brown sugar and pecans. Sprinkle over potatoes. Cover and microwave until hot, 6 to 7 minutes.

6 or 7 servings.

ORIENTAL SPINACH

10 to 12 ounces spinach, torn into
      bite-size pieces
 1 can (8½ ounces) water chestnuts,
      drained and sliced
 5 green onions, sliced
 2 tablespoons vegetable oil
 2 tablespoons vinegar
 2 tablespoons soy sauce
 1 teaspoon sugar

Cover and microwave spinach, water chestnuts
and onions until spinach is limp, 3 to 4 minutes;
stir.

Microwave oil, vinegar, soy sauce and sugar to
boiling, 1 to 1½ minutes. Pour over spinach;
toss.

6 servings.

CREAMED SPINACH
AND MUSHROOMS

 1 package (10 ounces) frozen chopped
      spinach
 2 tablespoons margarine or butter
 2 cans (4 ounces each) mushroom stems
      and pieces, drained
¼ cup chopped onion
 1 can (10¾ ounces) condensed cream of
      mushroom soup
¼ teaspoon salt
⅛ teaspoon Worcestershire sauce
      Dash of pepper

Microwave frozen spinach in package on paper
towel until thawed, 4 to 5 minutes; drain.

Cover and microwave margarine, mushrooms
and onion in 1-quart casserole until onion is
crisp-tender, 3 to 4 minutes.

Stir in spinach, soup, salt, Worcestershire sauce
and pepper. Cover and microwave 2 minutes;
stir. Cover and microwave until hot, 2 to 2½
minutes.

6 servings.

GOLDEN ORANGE
SQUASH BAKE

 2 packages (12 ounces each) frozen
      cooked squash
 2 tablespoons margarine or butter
 1 can (11 ounces) mandarin oranges,
      drained
¼ cup maple-flavored syrup

Place squash and margarine in 2-quart casserole or bowl. Cover with paper towel and
microwave until thawed, 11 to 12 minutes. Top
with orange segments; drizzle with syrup.
Microwave uncovered until hot, 4 to 5 minutes.

6 servings.

RAISIN-ORANGE
ACORN SQUASH

 1 medium acorn squash
 2 tablespoons margarine or butter
¼ cup raisins
½ teaspoon grated orange peel
¼ cup orange juice
 2 tablespoons packed brown sugar
¼ teaspoon salt

Prick squash in several places with fork.
Microwave on paper towel 4 minutes; turn
squash over. Microwave until just tender, 3 to 5
minutes. Let stand until cool enough to handle,
about 15 minutes.

Cut squash lengthwise into halves; remove
seeds and fibers. Place squash halves cut sides
up in serving dish. Divide margarine, raisins,
orange peel, orange juice, brown sugar and salt
between squash halves. Cover loosely and
microwave orange juice mixture to boiling, 4 to
5 minutes.

2 servings.

STUFFED TOMATOES

  6 medium tomatoes
  2 tablespoons margarine or butter
  2 tablespoons packed brown sugar
  1 slice bread, cubed
  ½ teaspoon salt
     Dash of pepper

Cut thin slice from stem end of each tomato. Scoop out pulp, leaving a ¼-inch wall; chop enough pulp to measure 1 cup.

Microwave margarine uncovered in 3-cup bowl until melted, 30 seconds to 1 minute. Stir in reserved tomato pulp, the sugar, bread cubes, salt and pepper. Spoon into tomatoes. Microwave uncovered until warm, 2½ to 3 minutes.

6 servings.

CHEESE-CRUMBED TOMATOES

  2 medium tomatoes
  1 tablespoon French dressing
  2 tablespoons crushed cheese crackers

Cut tomatoes into halves. Drizzle cut sides with dressing; sprinkle with crackers. Microwave uncovered 1 minute; turn dish one-quarter turn. Microwave until hot, 1½ to 2 minutes.

4 servings.

ZUCCHINI AND CORN

  3 medium zucchini, sliced
  ½ medium green pepper, cut into strips
  2 tablespoons water
  1 package (10 ounces) frozen corn
     in butter sauce
  ¼ teaspoon seasoned salt

Cover and microwave zucchini, green pepper and water in 2-quart casserole or bowl until zucchini is tender, 9 to 10 minutes; drain.

Cut small slit in corn pouch. Microwave corn until hot, 6 to 7 minutes.

Stir corn and salt into zucchini. Microwave uncovered until hot, 1 to 2 minutes.

6 servings.

STUFFED ZUCCHINI

  4 medium zucchini
  3 green onions, sliced
  2 tablespoons margarine or butter
  1 slice bread, cubed
  ¼ cup grated Parmesan cheese
  1 medium tomato, chopped
  ¼ teaspoon salt
     Dash of pepper

Cut zucchini lengthwise into halves. Scoop out pulp, leaving a ¼-inch wall; chop pulp and reserve. Place zucchini shells cut sides down. Cover loosely and microwave until crisp-tender, 5 to 6 minutes.

Cover and microwave reserved pulp, the onions and margarine in 1½-quart casserole or bowl until tender, 6 to 7 minutes. Stir in bread cubes, cheese, tomato, salt and pepper.

Turn zucchini shells cut sides up; spoon mixture into shells. Cover loosely and microwave until hot, 2 to 3 minutes.

8 servings.

SPINACH-RICE CASSEROLE

½ package (10-ounce size) frozen chopped spinach
1 cup instant rice
1½ cups milk
1 teaspoon salt
1 teaspoon instant minced onion
2 eggs, beaten

Cover and microwave frozen spinach in 1-quart casserole until thawed, 3 to 4 minutes. Stir in remaining ingredients.

Cover and microwave 7 minutes; turn casserole one-quarter turn. Microwave until knife inserted near center comes out clean, 2 to 4 minutes. Let stand a few minutes before serving.

5 or 6 servings.

STEAMED RICE

1 cup long-grain rice
2 cups water
1 tablespoon margarine or butter
½ teaspoon salt

Combine all ingredients in 3-quart casserole. Cover and microwave to boiling, 7 to 8½ minutes. Let stand 10 minutes; stir. Cover and microwave until rice is tender and liquid is absorbed, 3 to 5 minutes. Let stand 5 minutes.

4 servings.

CURRIED RICE

1 cup long-grain rice
2 cups water
4 green onions, sliced
2 tablespoons margarine or butter
1 teaspoon instant chicken bouillon
½ teaspoon salt
½ teaspoon curry powder

Combine all ingredients in 3-quart casserole. Cover and microwave to boiling, 7 to 8½ minutes. Let stand 10 minutes; stir. Cover and microwave until rice is tender and liquid is absorbed, 3 to 5 minutes. Let stand 5 minutes.

4 servings.

SPANISH RICE

2 slices bacon, cut into ½-inch pieces
1½ cups instant rice
½ cup chopped green pepper
1⅓ cups water
1 can (16 ounces) stewed tomatoes
1 teaspoon salt
1 teaspoon instant minced onion
½ teaspoon chili powder
¼ teaspoon dried oregano leaves
⅛ teaspoon pepper

Place bacon in 1½-quart casserole. Cover with paper towel and microwave until crisp, 2 to 3 minutes. Stir in remaining ingredients. Cover and microwave 5 minutes; stir. Cover and microwave until rice is tender, 5 to 6 minutes.

6 servings.

NOODLES ROMANOFF

2 cups noodles, cooked
1 cup dairy sour cream
2 tablespoons grated Parmesan cheese
2 tablespoons milk
1 tablespoon chopped chives
½ teaspoon salt
¼ teaspoon garlic salt
　Dash of pepper
2 tablespoons grated Parmesan cheese
¼ teaspoon paprika

Mix all ingredients except 2 tablespoons cheese and the paprika in 1-quart casserole. Mix cheese and paprika; sprinkle over noodles. Cover and microwave until hot, 5 to 6 minutes.

4 servings.

BAVARIAN-STYLE MACARONI

5 slices bacon
4 green onions, sliced
2 tablespoons sugar
1 tablespoon flour
1 teaspoon instant beef bouillon
½ teaspoon salt
　Dash of pepper
¼ cup vinegar
½ cup water
1½ cups macaroni, cooked

Place bacon in 1½-quart casserole. Cover with paper towel and microwave until crisp, 3½ to 4½ minutes. Remove bacon and drain on paper towel.

Stir green onions, sugar, flour, bouillon, salt, pepper, vinegar and water into bacon fat in casserole. Microwave uncovered until mixture boils and thickens, 3 to 4 minutes.

Stir in macaroni. Crumble bacon; sprinkle over top. Cover and microwave until hot, 3 to 4 minutes.

6 servings.

MICROWAVE TIPS

Breads heat and cook very quickly. A ring shape is often used to prevent the outside edge from overcooking before the center is cooked. Some bread doughs hold their shape and form their own ring shape, while others require a special dish with a tube center. You can make your own ring dish by simply placing a straight-sided beverage glass in the center of a round casserole or baking dish.

Though special muffin pans for microwaving are available, you can do-it-yourself by placing paper-lined custard or coffee cups in a circle on a large glass plate.

PARMESAN-BUTTERED ROLLS

¼ cup margarine or butter, softened
2 tablespoons grated Parmesan cheese
1 teaspoon dried parsley flakes
¼ teaspoon garlic salt
6 to 8 dinner rolls

Combine margarine, cheese, parsley flakes and garlic salt. Cut each roll crosswise ⅔ of the way to bottom. Spoon or spread about 1 rounded teaspoon margarine mixture on cut surface of each roll. Microwave uncovered until warm, 30 seconds to 1 minute.

6 to 8 rolls.

ONIONY FRENCH BREAD

⅓ cup margarine or butter, softened
4 green onions, thinly sliced
   (about 2 tablespoons)
1 loaf (16 ounces) French bread

Combine margarine and onions. Cut loaf crosswise in half. Slice each horizontally, cutting almost through. Spread cut sides with onion butter. Microwave, one half-loaf at a time, on paper towel until hot, 45 seconds to 1 minute.

BROWN BREAD

½ cup all-purpose flour
½ cup cornmeal
½ cup whole wheat flour
½ cup raisins
1 teaspoon baking soda
½ teaspoon salt
1 egg
1 cup buttermilk
⅓ cup molasses
1 tablespoon vegetable oil

Lightly grease 1½-quart casserole. Place small straight-sided beverage glass, 2 inches in diameter, open end up in center of casserole. Mix all ingredients. Pour batter into casserole.

Microwave uncovered 4 minutes; turn casserole one-quarter turn. Microwave until no longer doughy, 1½ to 2½ minutes. Let stand 10 minutes. Twist and remove glass; invert bread on serving plate.

6 to 8 servings.

CORN MUFFINS

½ cup biscuit baking mix
¼ cup yellow cornmeal
2 teaspoons sugar
⅛ teaspoon salt
¼ cup milk
2 teaspoons vegetable oil
1 egg
   Corn flakes, crushed

Mix baking mix, cornmeal, sugar and salt. Beat milk, oil and egg. Stir into dry ingredients just until moistened. Spoon into 5 paper-lined plastic muffin cups or custard or coffee cups, filling ½ full. Sprinkle lightly with corn flakes.

Microwave 1½ minutes. Rotate or rearrange cups and microwave until no longer doughy, 30 seconds to 1 minute. Immediately remove from cups.

5 muffins.

BANANA-BRAN MUFFINS

½ cup milk
¾ cup wheat bran cereal
1 egg
1 medium banana, mashed (about ½ cup)
2 tablespoons vegetable oil
¾ cup all-purpose flour
¼ cup sugar
1 teaspoon baking powder
½ teaspoon salt

Mix milk and cereal; let stand 2 to 3 minutes. Beat in egg, banana and oil. Stir in flour, sugar, baking powder and salt. Spoon into 6 paper-lined plastic muffin cups or custard or coffee cups, filling ½ full.

Microwave uncovered 1½ minutes. Rotate or rearrange cups and microwave until no longer doughy, 30 seconds to 1 minute. Immediately remove from cups. Repeat with remaining batter.

12 muffins.

CINNAMON-SUGAR BLUEBERRY MUFFINS

1 package (13.5 ounces) blueberry muffin mix
½ cup milk
1 egg
2 tablespoons margarine or butter
3 tablespoons sugar
½ teaspoon ground cinnamon

Prepare muffin mix batter as directed on package. Spoon into 6 paper-lined plastic muffin cups or custard or coffee cups, filling ½ full. Microwave uncovered 1½ minutes. Rotate or rearrange cups and microwave until no longer doughy, 30 seconds to 1 minute. Repeat with remaining batter.

Microwave margarine uncovered in small dish until melted, 30 seconds to 1 minute. Mix sugar and cinnamon. Dip tops of muffins in melted margarine, then in cinnamon-sugar mixture.

12 muffins.

CARAMEL BISCUIT RING

3 tablespoons margarine or butter
⅓ cup packed brown sugar
1 tablespoon water
¼ cup chopped nuts
1½ cups biscuit baking mix
⅓ cup water

Microwave margarine, brown sugar and water uncovered in round baking dish, 8 x 1½ inches, 2 to 2½ minutes. Stir in nuts.

Stir biscuit mix and water until a soft dough forms. Drop dough by spoonfuls around side of baking dish, forming a ring. Spoon some of the caramel mixture from center over each biscuit.

Cover with paper towel and microwave 1½ minutes; turn dish one-quarter turn. Microwave until no longer doughy, 30 seconds to 1 minute. Cool 2 minutes; invert on serving plate.

4 or 5 servings.

MINI STREUSEL COFFEE CAKES

¼ cup margarine or butter, softened
¾ cup sugar
¾ cup milk
1 egg
1½ cups all-purpose flour
1½ teaspoons baking powder
¾ teaspoon salt
Streusel Topping (below)

Mix margarine, sugar, milk and egg. Stir in flour, baking powder and salt. Spoon into 6 paper-lined plastic muffin cups or custard or coffee cups, filling ½ full. Spoon rounded teaspoonful Streusel Topping onto each muffin.

Microwave 1½ minutes. Rotate or rearrange cups and microwave until no longer doughy, 30 seconds to 1 minute. Immediately remove from cups. Repeat with remaining batter and topping.

14 to 16 coffee cakes.

NOTE: For 2 to 4 muffins, microwave 45 seconds. Rotate or rearrange cups and microwave 30 seconds to 1 minute.

STREUSEL TOPPING

¼ cup packed brown sugar
2 tablespoons flour
2 teaspoons ground cinnamon
2 tablespoons firm margarine or butter

Mix all ingredients until crumbly.

DESSERTS

FRUIT AND DUMPLINGS

1 package (10 ounces) frozen raspberries, thawed
1 can (16 ounces) sliced pears
2 tablespoons cornstarch
1 teaspoon ground cinnamon
⅓ cup sugar
¾ cup biscuit baking mix
2 tablespoons sugar
¼ cup dairy sour cream
1 egg

Drain syrups from fruits into 4-cup glass measure; add enough water to measure 1½ cups. Stir in cornstarch, cinnamon and ⅓ cup sugar. Microwave 2 minutes; stir. Microwave until mixture boils and thickens, 2 to 3 minutes. Combine with fruits in round baking dish, 8 x 1½ inches.

Mix biscuit mix, 2 tablespoons sugar, the sour cream and egg; spoon onto fruit mixture, forming a ring around edge of dish. (Topping will cook toward center.) Spoon some of fruit sauce over topping. Microwave uncovered 3 minutes; turn dish one-quarter turn. Microwave until topping is no longer doughy, 3½ to 4½ minutes.

5 or 6 servings.

CRUNCHY BLUEBERRY DELIGHT

½ cup margarine or butter
1⅓ cups flaked coconut
1 cup all-purpose flour
¾ cup packed brown sugar
⅔ cup graham cracker crumbs (about 9 squares)
1 package (20 ounces) frozen unsweetened blueberries (about 4 cups)
¾ cup granulated sugar
3 tablespoons cornstarch
½ cup water

Microwave margarine uncovered in square baking dish, 8 x 8 x 2 inches, until melted, 30 seconds to 1 minute. Stir in coconut, flour, brown sugar and cracker crumbs. Microwave uncovered until lightly toasted, 5 to 7 minutes, stirring every 2 minutes. Reserve ¾ cup coconut mixture for topping; press remaining mixture firmly and evenly in baking dish.

Mix blueberries, granulated sugar and cornstarch in 2-quart casserole or bowl. Gradually stir in water. Cover and microwave until mixture boils and thickens, 11 to 12 minutes, stirring every 4 minutes. Cool slightly.

Spoon blueberries over coconut crust. Sprinkle with reserved coconut mixture. Refrigerate until set, 2 to 4 hours. Cut into squares.

9 servings.

REFRESHING RHUBARB DESSERT

½ cup margarine or butter
1 cup rolled oats
¾ cup all-purpose flour
⅔ cup packed brown sugar
1 teaspoon ground cinnamon
4 cups sliced rhubarb
1 cup granulated sugar
¾ cup orange juice
2 tablespoons cornstarch

Microwave margarine uncovered in round baking dish, 8 x 1½ inches, until melted, 30 seconds to 1 minute. Stir in rolled oats, flour, brown sugar and cinnamon. Microwave uncovered 1 minute; stir. Microwave uncovered until well coated, 1 to 1½ minutes. Reserve half of the oat mixture; press remaining mixture firmly and evenly in baking dish. Add rhubarb.

Mix granulated sugar, orange juice and cornstarch in 4-cup glass measure. Microwave 1 minute; stir. Microwave to boiling, 1 to 2 minutes. Pour over rhubarb. Sprinkle with reserved oat mixture. Microwave uncovered until rhubarb is tender, 7 to 8 minutes; cool.

6 to 8 servings.

RHUBARB CRUNCH

4 cups sliced fresh rhubarb (about 1 pound)
1 cup sugar
⅛ teaspoon almond extract
¼ cup margarine or butter
4 slices bread, cut into ¼-inch cubes
¼ cup sugar
½ cup chopped almonds
1 teaspoon grated orange peel

Mix rhubarb and 1 cup sugar in 2½-quart casserole. Cover and microwave until rhubarb is tender, 7 to 9 minutes. Stir in almond extract. Cool rhubarb sauce.

Microwave margarine uncovered in 10-inch pie plate until melted, 30 seconds to 1 minute. Stir in bread cubes, ¼ cup sugar and the almonds until well coated with margarine. Microwave uncovered until toasted, 7 to 8 minutes, stirring every 2 minutes. Stir in orange peel. To serve, spoon rhubarb sauce into dessert dishes; top with toasted bread mixture.

6 servings.

APPLESAUCE CRUNCH

Substitute 2½ to 3 cups applesauce for the cooked rhubarb sauce.

MICROWAVE TIP

Brown sugar and spices like nutmeg and cinnamon do double duty for microwaved desserts. Each gives its own special flavoring and, at the same time, adds a dash of color. This is particularly welcome for those dishes that would have a brown appearance when baked in a conventional oven.

EASY POACHED PEARS

4 fresh pears, cut into halves and cored
1 orange, pared and sectioned
2 tablespoons margarine or butter
⅓ cup honey
⅓ cup sweet white wine
1 package (3 ounces) cream cheese
   Ground nutmeg

Arrange pear halves cut sides up in oblong baking dish, 12 x 7½ x 2 inches. Place an orange section in each pear half. Dot each with margarine; drizzle with honey and wine. Cover loosely and microwave 3 minutes; turn dish one-half turn. Microwave until pears are tender, 3 to 4 minutes.

Microwave cream cheese uncovered in bowl until softened, about 30 seconds. Beat until fluffy. Spoon onto each pear half; sprinkle with nutmeg.

8 servings.

SUGAR-BAKED APPLES

⅔ cup sugar
⅓ cup all-purpose flour
1 teaspoon ground cinnamon
¼ cup margarine or butter
2 tablespoons raisins
4 cooking apples, cut into halves and cored
⅓ cup orange juice

Mix sugar, flour and cinnamon; cut in margarine until crumbly. Stir in raisins.

Arrange apples cut sides up in round baking dish, 8 x 1½ inches. Spoon crumb mixture over apples. Drizzle with orange juice. Cover loosely and microwave 4½ minutes; turn dish one-quarter turn. Microwave until apples are tender, 2½ to 3½ minutes.

8 servings.

APPLE CRUMB DESSERT

4 cups sliced pared apples (about 4 medium)
½ teaspoon ground cinnamon
1 cup all-purpose flour
¼ cup granulated sugar
¼ cup packed brown sugar
¼ teaspoon salt
¼ teaspoon baking soda
1 egg
¼ cup packed brown sugar
⅓ cup margarine or butter

Arrange apples in square baking dish, 8 x 8 x 2 inches. Sprinkle with cinnamon. Mix flour, granulated sugar, ¼ cup brown sugar, the salt, baking soda and egg with fork until crumbly. Spoon over apples. Sprinkle with ¼ cup brown sugar.

Microwave margarine uncovered until melted, 30 seconds to 1 minute; drizzle over apples. Microwave uncovered until apples are tender, 10 to 12 minutes. Serve warm and, if desired, with cream.

6 servings.

FRUIT STREUSEL

1 can (21 ounces) cherry pie filling
1 can (8¾ ounces) sliced peaches
½ package (18.5-ounce size) yellow cake mix (about 2 cups)
½ cup chopped nuts
½ teaspoon ground cinnamon
⅓ cup margarine or butter

Mix pie filling and peaches (with syrup) in ungreased 2-quart casserole. Sprinkle cake mix (dry), nuts and cinnamon onto fruit mixture.

Microwave margarine uncovered until melted, 30 seconds to 1 minute; drizzle over topping. Microwave uncovered until bubbly and topping is almost firm, 11 to 13 minutes, rotating casserole every 4 minutes.

6 to 8 servings.

MERINGUE-TOPPED RICE PUDDING

 1 package (3⅛ ounces) vanilla regular
   pudding and pie filling
 ½ cup uncooked instant rice
 ½ cup raisins
 3 cups milk
 2 eggs, separated
 ¼ teaspoon cream of tartar
 ¼ cup sugar
 ½ teaspoon vanilla
   Ground nutmeg

Mix pudding and pie filling (dry), rice, raisins and milk in ungreased 1½-quart casserole. Cover and microwave 4 minutes; stir. Microwave uncovered to boiling, 3½ to 4½ minutes.

Beat egg yolks; gradually beat in about 1 cup of the hot pudding. Blend into pudding in casserole. Microwave uncovered just until edges are bubbly, 1 to 1½ minutes. Cool 10 minutes.

Beat egg whites and cream of tartar until foamy. Beat in sugar, 1 tablespoon at a time; continue beating until stiff peaks form. Beat in vanilla. Spoon meringue onto pudding in 6 to 8 mounds. Microwave uncovered until meringue is set, 2 to 2½ minutes. Sprinkle with nutmeg.

6 to 8 servings.

MINCEMEAT STEAMED PUDDING

 2 tablespoons margarine or butter, softened
 ½ cup packed brown sugar
 2 eggs
 1 cup prepared mincemeat
 ⅓ cup milk
 1¼ cups all-purpose flour
 1½ teaspoons baking powder
 ½ cup chopped nuts
   Rum Sauce (below)

Grease round baking dish, 8 x 1½ inches. Place straight-sided beverage glass or custard cup open end up in center of baking dish. Mix margarine, brown sugar and eggs. Stir in mincemeat and milk. Mix in flour, baking powder and nuts. Spoon batter around glass in baking dish.

Cover tightly with tent of plastic wrap and microwave until cake around glass is no longer doughy, 5 to 6 minutes, rotating dish every 2 minutes. Cool 5 minutes. Uncover and twist glass out; invert pudding onto serving plate. Serve warm with Rum Sauce.

8 to 10 servings.

NOTE: Pudding can be microwaved in greased 5-cup ring dish. Microwave and cool as directed above.

RUM SAUCE

 ¾ cup whipping cream
 ¼ cup milk
 ¾ cup sugar
 1 tablespoon cornstarch
 ½ cup margarine or butter
 1 teaspoon rum flavoring or 1 tablespoon rum

Mix whipping cream, milk, sugar and cornstarch in 4-cup glass measure. Add margarine. Microwave 3 minutes; stir. Microwave to boiling, 1 to 2 minutes. Stir in rum.

RAISIN BREAD PUDDING

- 3 tablespoons margarine or butter
- 4 slices bread, cubed
- ½ cup packed brown sugar
- ⅓ cup raisins
- 2 cups milk
- 3 eggs, slightly beaten
  Ground nutmeg

Microwave margarine uncovered in 1-quart casserole until melted, 30 seconds to 1 minute. Stir in bread cubes, brown sugar and raisins.

Microwave milk in 4-cup glass measure until steaming hot, 4½ to 5 minutes. Beat in eggs. Pour over bread mixture. Sprinkle with nutmeg.

Pour 1 cup warm water into square baking dish, 8 x 8 x 2 inches; place casserole in baking dish. Microwave uncovered 6 minutes; turn dish one-quarter turn. Microwave until center is just about set, 8 to 10 minutes. Spoon liquid in bottom of casserole over each serving.

6 servings.

CHERRY-BROWNIE PUDDING CAKE

- 2 squares (1 ounce each) unsweetened chocolate
- ¼ cup margarine or butter
- 1 cup sugar
- ½ teaspoon vanilla
- 2 eggs
- 1 can (21 ounces) cherry pie filling
- 1 cup all-purpose flour
- ½ teaspoon baking powder
- ½ teaspoon salt
- ¼ cup water
- 2 tablespoons margarine or butter

Microwave chocolate and ¼ cup margarine uncovered in bowl until melted, 1½ to 2 minutes.

Beat in sugar, vanilla and eggs. Stir in 1 cup of the pie filling, the flour, baking powder and salt.

Stir together remaining pie filling, the water and 2 tablespoons margarine in ungreased square baking dish, 8 x 8 x 2 inches. Microwave uncovered until margarine is melted, 1 to 2 minutes; stir.

Spoon brownie mixture over cherries. Microwave uncovered 10 minutes; turn dish one-quarter turn. Microwave until top springs back when touched lightly, 4 to 5 minutes. (Topping will look moist.)

8 or 9 servings.

COCONUT PUDDING CAKE

- 1 cup packed brown sugar
- 1¼ cups water
- ¼ cup chopped nuts
- 2 tablespoons margarine or butter
- 1 cup all-purpose flour
- 2 tablespoons unsweetened cocoa
- 1½ teaspoons baking powder
- ½ teaspoon salt
- 1 teaspoon vanilla
- ½ cup flaked coconut
- ½ cup milk

Microwave brown sugar and water uncovered in square baking dish, 8 x 8 x 2 inches, until hot, 2 to 2½ minutes. Stir until sugar is dissolved. Sprinkle with nuts.

Microwave margarine uncovered in bowl until softened, 15 to 45 seconds. Stir in remaining ingredients. Spoon onto mixture in baking dish. Microwave uncovered 4 minutes; turn dish one-quarter turn. Microwave until top appears almost dry, 4 to 5 minutes.

6 servings.

NOODLE PUDDING

- 1 package (8 ounces) cream cheese
- 1/3 cup sugar
- 2 eggs, beaten
- 1/4 teaspoon salt
- 1/4 teaspoon ground nutmeg
- 1/4 cup raisins
- 2 cups noodles, cooked
  Ground nutmeg
  Sweetened fruit (strawberries, blueberries, raspberries)

Microwave cream cheese uncovered in round baking dish, 8 x 1½ inches, until softened, 45 seconds to 1 minute; beat until smooth. Beat in sugar and eggs. Stir in salt, ¼ teaspoon nutmeg, the raisins and noodles. Spread evenly in baking dish; sprinkle with nutmeg.

Microwave uncovered 3 minutes; turn dish one-quarter turn. Microwave until center is just about set, 2 to 3 minutes. Refrigerate until set, at least 1 hour. Cut into wedges and serve with sweetened fruit.

6 to 8 servings.

MOCHA FROZEN CREME

- 1/3 cup milk
- 1 teaspoon instant coffee
- 1 cup miniature marshmallows
- 1/2 cup semisweet chocolate chips
- 1/4 cup chopped almonds
- 1 tablespoon brandy (optional)
- 1/2 teaspoon vanilla
- 2 tablespoons sugar
- 1 cup chilled whipping cream

Mix milk and coffee in 4-cup glass measure. Add marshmallows and chocolate chips. Microwave to boiling, 1½ to 2 minutes; stir until smooth. Stir in almonds, brandy and vanilla; cool.

Beat whipping cream and sugar in chilled bowl until stiff. Fold chocolate mixture into whipped cream. Spoon into 8 paper-lined muffin cups. Freeze until firm, about 4 hours. To serve, peel off papers and, if desired, top each with additional whipped cream and a maraschino cherry.

8 servings.

FROZEN RASPBERRY SQUARES

- 1/3 cup margarine or butter
- 1 cup all-purpose flour
- 1/4 cup packed brown sugar
- 1 pint raspberry sherbet
- 1 quart vanilla ice cream
- 1 package (10 ounces) frozen raspberries, thawed
- 2 tablespoons granulated sugar
- 1 tablespoon cornstarch

Microwave margarine uncovered in square baking dish, 8 x 8 x 2 inches, until melted, 30 seconds to 1 minute. Stir in flour and brown sugar. Microwave until light brown, 3 to 4 minutes, stirring every minute. Reserve ⅓ cup crumb mixture for topping; press remaining mixture firmly and evenly in baking dish. Cool.

Spoon and spread sherbet in layer on crumb crust; top with ice cream layer. Sprinkle with reserved crumb mixture. Cover and freeze until firm, at least 6 to 8 hours.

Drain liquid from raspberries into 2-cup glass measure; add enough water to measure 1 cup. Stir in granulated sugar and cornstarch. Microwave 2 minutes; stir. Microwave to boiling, 30 seconds to 1½ minutes. Stir in raspberries. Refrigerate until ready to serve. Cut dessert into squares; serve with raspberry sauce.

9 servings.

ICE CREAM WITH BUTTERSCOTCH SAUCE

⅔ cup packed brown sugar
⅓ cup corn syrup
¼ cup margarine or butter
¼ cup milk
½ teaspoon vanilla
   Ice cream (vanilla, butter pecan, coffee)

Mix brown sugar, corn syrup, margarine and milk in 4-cup glass measure. Microwave 1½ minutes; stir. Microwave to a rapid boil, 1 to 1½ minutes. Stir in vanilla. Serve over ice cream. Cover and refrigerate any leftover sauce. Microwave until warm, 1 to 1½ minutes.

DATE CHEESECAKE SQUARES

1 package (14 ounces) date bar mix
½ cup hot water
1 tablespoon plus 2 teaspoons cold water
1 package (8 ounces) cream cheese
1 tablespoon sugar
1 tablespoon milk
½ teaspoon lemon juice

Mix Date Mix and hot water. Empty Crumb Mix into square baking dish, 8 x 8 x 2 inches. Add cold water; stir with fork until blended. Microwave uncovered until light brown, 4½ to 5 minutes, stirring every 2 minutes. Stir to break up mixture. Cool slightly. Reserve ⅓ cup crumb mixture; press remaining mixture firmly and evenly in baking dish. Spoon date filling onto base, spreading evenly. Microwave uncovered 2 minutes; turn dish one-quarter turn. Microwave until set around edge, 1 to 1½ minutes.

Microwave cream cheese uncovered in 3-cup bowl until softened, 45 seconds to 1 minute. Beat in sugar, milk and lemon juice. Spoon onto date filling; sprinkle with reserved crumb mixture. Refrigerate until firm, 2 to 3 hours. Cut into squares.

9 servings.

PUMPKIN SQUARES

¼ cup margarine or butter
½ cup all-purpose flour
¼ cup packed brown sugar
¼ cup rolled oats
1 envelope unflavored gelatin
¼ cup cold water
1 can (16 ounces) pumpkin
2 eggs
1 cup evaporated milk
¾ cup packed brown sugar
1 teaspoon ground cinnamon
½ teaspoon salt
¼ teaspoon ground ginger
¼ teaspoon ground cloves
   Whipped cream

Microwave margarine uncovered in square baking dish, 8 x 8 x 2 inches, until melted, 30 seconds to 1 minute. Stir in flour, ¼ cup brown sugar and the oats. Microwave uncovered 1½ minutes; stir. Microwave uncovered until light brown, 1½ to 2 minutes. Press mixture firmly and evenly in baking dish.

Sprinkle gelatin on cold water in 2½-quart casserole or bowl to soften. Beat in pumpkin, eggs, evaporated milk, ¾ cup brown sugar, the cinnamon, salt, ginger and cloves.

Microwave uncovered 4 minutes; stir. Microwave uncovered until thickened, 4 to 4½ minutes, stirring every minute. Pour onto crust. Microwave uncovered 2 minutes; turn dish one-quarter turn. Microwave 3 minutes. Refrigerate until set, 2 to 3 hours. Serve with whipped cream.

9 servings.

CHOCO-MINT DESSERT SQUARES

2 tablespoons margarine or butter
13 creme-filled chocolate cookies, finely crushed (about 1⅓ cups)
1 cup boiling water
1 package (3 ounces) lime-flavored gelatin
1 package (8 ounces) cream cheese
¾ cup sugar
2 or 3 drops green food color (optional)
1 cup whipping cream, whipped
¾ cup chocolate-flavored ice-cream topping
½ teaspoon peppermint extract

Microwave margarine uncovered in oblong baking dish, 12 x 7½ x 2 inches, until melted, 30 seconds to 1 minute. Stir in cookie crumbs. Press mixture firmly and evenly in baking dish; refrigerate.

Pour boiling water over gelatin, stirring until gelatin is dissolved. Cool 30 minutes.

Microwave cream cheese uncovered in 2½-quart casserole or bowl until softened, 45 seconds to 1 minute. Beat in sugar until smooth. Gradually beat in gelatin mixture and food color. Fold in whipped cream. Pour over crumb crust. Refrigerate until set, at least 4 hours.

Combine ice-cream topping and peppermint extract. Cut dessert into squares; serve with chocolate sauce.

15 servings.

CHOCOLATE-CREAM CAKE DESSERT

½ package (18.5-ounce size) yellow cake mix (about 2 cups)
⅔ cup sugar
1 envelope unflavored gelatin
⅛ teaspoon salt
1¼ cups milk
2 squares (1 ounce each) unsweetened chocolate
2 eggs, beaten
1 teaspoon vanilla
1 cup chilled whipping cream

Grease bottom only of oblong baking dish, 12 x 7½ x 2 inches. Prepare cake mix for 1 layer as directed on package. Pour batter into baking dish; spread evenly. Microwave uncovered 4 minutes; turn dish one-half turn. Microwave until wooden pick inserted near center comes out clean, 2½ to 3½ minutes. (Parts of the cake will appear very moist, but these parts will continue to cook while standing.) Cool thoroughly. Cut into 1-inch squares.

Mix sugar, gelatin and salt in 1-quart casserole or bowl. Gradually stir in milk. Add chocolate. Microwave uncovered to boiling, 4 to 5 minutes, stirring every 2 minutes. Beat until mixture is smooth.

Gradually stir a small amount of the hot mixture into eggs. Blend into hot mixture in casserole. Stir in vanilla; cool.

Beat whipping cream in 4-quart bowl until very soft peaks form. Fold in chocolate mixture; then fold in cake squares. Spoon into dessert dishes. Refrigerate until set, at least 2 hours.

12 servings.

CHOCOLATE CHEESECAKE

3 tablespoons margarine or butter
1 cup graham cracker crumbs
1 package (8 ounces) cream cheese
¼ cup sugar
1 tablespoon plus 1½ teaspoons
   unsweetened cocoa
1 egg
1 teaspoon vanilla
1 cup dairy sour cream
3 tablespoons sugar
¼ teaspoon almond extract

Microwave margarine uncovered in round bak-ing dish, 8 x 1½ inches, until melted, 45 seconds to 1 minute. Stir in cracker crumbs. Press mixture firmly and evenly in bottom and 1 inch up side of dish.

Microwave cream cheese uncovered in bowl until softened, 30 seconds to 1 minute. Blend in ¼ cup sugar and the cocoa. Beat in egg and vanilla. Pour into crust. Microwave uncovered 1½ minutes; turn dish one-quarter turn. Microwave until set around edge, 1 to 2 minutes.

Mix sour cream, 3 tablespoons sugar and the almond extract. Spoon over cream cheese layer, spreading to cover. Microwave uncovered until topping is warm, 1½ to 2 minutes. Re-frigerate at least 2 hours.

FRESH STRAWBERRY-RHUBARB PIE

1½ cups all-purpose flour
½ teaspoon salt
½ cup shortening
3 to 4 tablespoons cold water
3 cups ¼-inch slices rhubarb
1 pint fresh strawberries, cut into halves
1⅓ cups sugar
¼ cup cornstarch
2 tablespoons margarine or butter

Mix flour and salt; cut in shortening thoroughly. Sprinkle in water, 1 tablespoon at a time, mixing until flour is moistened and pastry almost cleans side of bowl.

Gather pastry into a ball. Reserve ¼ of the pastry; shape remaining pastry into flattened round on lightly floured cloth-covered board. Roll 2 inches larger than inverted 9-inch pie plate. Fold pastry into quarters; place in pie plate. Unfold pastry and ease into plate. Trim over-hanging edge of pastry 1 inch from rim of plate. Fold and roll pastry under, even with plate; flute. Prick bottom and side thoroughly with fork.

Microwave uncovered 2½ minutes; turn plate one-quarter turn. Microwave until crust has a dry, flaky appearance, 1½ to 2½ minutes.

Roll reserved pastry to 8-inch circle; place on a paper towel. Cut into 6 or 8 wedges. If desired, sprinkle with about 1 teaspoon cinnamon-sugar. Microwave uncovered until crust has a dry, flaky appearance, 2 to 3 minutes. Remove from paper towel; cool.

Mix remaining ingredients in 2-quart casserole. Cover and microwave 5 minutes; stir. Micro-wave uncovered until mixture boils and thick-ens, 6 to 8 minutes, stirring every 2 minutes. Cool slightly, about 30 minutes. Pour into pie shell; top with pastry wedges. Cool. Serve with ice cream if desired.

FROSTY CHOCOLATE-CARAMEL PIE

    Graham Cracker Crust (below)
1 package (6 ounces) semisweet chocolate chips
3 tablespoons water
1 teaspoon vanilla
1 container (9 ounces) frozen whipped topping, thawed (about 4 cups)
28 caramel candies
¼ cup water
⅓ cup pecan halves

Prepare and microwave Graham Cracker Crust. Microwave chocolate chips and 3 tablespoons water uncovered in 2½-quart bowl or casserole until chocolate is softened, 1 to 1½ minutes. Stir until smooth; let stand 10 minutes. Stir in vanilla; fold in whipped topping. Spoon into crust. Freeze until firm, at least 4 hours.

Microwave caramel candies and ¼ cup water in 4-cup glass measure until candies are softened, 1½ to 2½ minutes. Stir until smooth. Stir in pecans; cool. Serve over pie.

GRAHAM CRACKER CRUST

¼ cup margarine or butter
1¼ cups graham cracker crumbs (about 15 squares)
2 tablespoons sugar

Microwave margarine uncovered in 9-inch pie plate until melted, 30 seconds to 1 minute. Stir in graham cracker crumbs and sugar. Microwave uncovered 45 seconds; turn plate one-quarter turn. Microwave until lightly browned, 45 seconds to 1½ minutes.

MICROWAVED PIE SHELL

Prepare pastry for 9-inch One-Crust Pie as directed on package of pie crust sticks or mix except—prick bottom and side with fork. Microwave uncovered 2 minutes; turn dish one-half turn. Microwave until crust has a dry, flaky appearance, 2 to 3 minutes.

PUMPKIN MERINGUE PIE

    9-inch Microwaved Pie Shell (above)
2 eggs, separated
1 can (13 ounces) evaporated milk (about 1⅔ cups)
1 package (4½ ounces) egg custard mix
1 can (16 ounces) pumpkin
¼ cup packed brown sugar
¾ teaspoon ground cinnamon
¼ teaspoon ground nutmeg
¼ teaspoon ground cloves
⅛ teaspoon ground ginger
¼ teaspoon cream of tartar
¼ cup granulated sugar

Prepare and microwave pie shell. Beat egg yolks in 2½-quart casserole or bowl. Beat in remaining ingredients except egg whites, cream of tartar and granulated sugar. Microwave uncovered to boiling, 7 to 8 minutes, stirring every 2 minutes. Pour into pie shell.

Beat egg whites and cream of tartar until foamy. Beat in granulated sugar, 1 tablespoon at a time, until stiff peaks form. Spread meringue around edge of pie. Microwave uncovered until meringue is set, 1½ to 2 minutes. Refrigerate until set, at least 4 hours.

PEACHES AND CREAM PIE

9 - inch Microwaved Pie Shell (page 50)
3 tablespoons cornstarch
¾ cup sugar
1½ cups water
1 package (3 ounces) peach-flavored gelatin
½ teaspoon almond extract
2 cups sliced peaches (about 4 medium)*
2 cups sweetened whipped cream or whipped topping

Prepare and microwave pie shell. Mix cornstarch, sugar and water in 1-quart casserole or bowl. Microwave uncovered 2 minutes; stir. Microwave uncovered until mixture boils and thickens, 2 to 2½ minutes. Stir in gelatin and extract. Cool 30 minutes.

Arrange peaches in pie shell. Top with gelatin mixture. Refrigerate until set, 3 to 4 hours. Just before serving, top pie with whipped cream.

*1 can (16 ounces) peach slices, drained, can be substituted for the fresh peaches. Use drained syrup for part of the water.

BLUEBERRY CREAM PIE

9 - inch Microwaved Pie Shell (page 50)
1 package (20 ounces) frozen blueberries (about 4 cups)
¾ cup sugar
3 tablespoons cornstarch
½ cup water
1 package (8 ounces) cream cheese
1 container (9 ounces) frozen whipped topping, thawed (about 4 cups)

Prepare and microwave pie shell. Combine frozen blueberries and sugar in 1-quart casserole or bowl. Cover and microwave 2 minutes; stir. Cover and microwave until berries are thawed, 2 to 3 minutes.

Mix cornstarch and water in 2-cup glass measure. Spoon in juice from berries. Microwave 1 minute; stir. Microwave until mixture boils and thickens, 1 to 1½ minutes. Stir into berries; cool 15 minutes.

Microwave cream cheese uncovered in 2½-quart casserole or bowl until softened, 45 seconds to 1 minute. Beat until smooth. Reserve 1 cup of the berry mixture; fold remainder into cream cheese. Stir in whipped topping. Spoon into pie shell. Top with reserved berry mixture. Refrigerate until set, 2 to 3 hours.

PECAN TARTS

3 eggs
1 cup sugar
1 cup corn syrup
⅓ cup margarine or butter
½ cup chopped pecans
1 teaspoon vanilla
2 packages (5 ounces each) baked pastry shells (3-inch size)
Whipped cream (optional)

Beat eggs, sugar and corn syrup in 2-quart casserole or bowl. Add margarine and pecans. Microwave uncovered until mixture boils and thickens slightly, 5 to 7 minutes, stirring every 2 minutes. Stir in vanilla.

Remove pastry shells from foil pans; place 6 shells on a plate. Pour filling into shells. Microwave uncovered, 1 plate at a time, until filling starts to bubble, 30 seconds to 1 minute. Refrigerate until ready to serve. Top with whipped cream.

12 tarts.

EASY NAPOLEONS

1¾ cups milk
1 package (3⅛ ounces) vanilla regular pudding and pie filling
1 package (3 ounces) cream cheese
1 package (11 ounces) pie crust sticks or mix
1 can (21 ounces) cherry pie filling

Mix milk and pudding and pie filling (dry) in 4-cup glass measure. Microwave 4 minutes; stir. Microwave to boiling, 1 to 2 minutes. Microwave cream cheese in 3-cup bowl until softened, 30 to 45 seconds. Slowly blend 1 cup of the pudding mixture into cream cheese; stir into pudding mixture in glass measure. Cover and refrigerate.

Prepare pastry for 2-crust pie as directed on package. Roll half of the dough on floured surface into rectangle, 15 x 9 inches. Cut into 9 rectangles, 5 x 3 inches; prick each with a fork. Repeat with remaining dough. Arrange 6 rectangles on double thickness of paper towels placed on piece of cardboard or a plastic cutting board. Microwave uncovered 1½ minutes. Turn paper towel one-quarter turn. Microwave until pastry has a dry, flaky appearance, 1 to 1½ minutes. Immediately remove from paper towels; cool. Repeat with remaining rectangles.

To serve, top 9 rectangles with half of the pudding mixture, then with half of the pie filling. Top with remaining pastry rectangles, pudding mixture and pie filling.

9 servings.

CHOCOLATE MACAROON CAKE

1 cup all-purpose flour
¾ cup sugar
¼ cup unsweetened cocoa
½ teaspoon baking soda
¼ teaspoon salt
½ teaspoon vanilla
¼ cup shortening
¾ cup buttermilk
1 egg
  Macaroon Filling (below)
  Chocolate Frosting (below)

Grease bottom only of oblong baking dish, 10 x 6 x 1½ inches. Blend all ingredients except Macaroon Filling and Chocolate Frosting in large mixer bowl on low speed, scraping bowl constantly. Beat 3 minutes on high speed, scraping bowl occasionally. Pour batter evenly into baking dish. Spoon Macaroon Filling onto batter by teaspoonfuls.

Microwave uncovered 5 minutes; turn dish one-half turn. Microwave until wooden pick inserted in center comes out clean, 3 to 4 minutes. (Parts of the cake will appear very moist, but these parts will continue to cook while standing.) Cool thoroughly; frost with Chocolate Frosting.

MACAROON FILLING

1 cup flaked or grated coconut
¼ cup corn syrup
1 tablespoon flour
1 tablespoon milk
½ teaspoon almond extract

Mix all ingredients.

CHOCOLATE FROSTING

2 cups powdered sugar
2 tablespoons unsweetened cocoa
3 tablespoons margarine or butter, softened
½ teaspoon vanilla
2 to 3 tablespoons milk or water

Mix powdered sugar, cocoa and margarine. Stir in vanilla. Beat in milk, 1 teaspoon at a time, until smooth and of spreading consistency.

NUTMEG CAKE

1½ cups all-purpose flour
1½ cups packed brown sugar
 ⅓ cup margarine or butter
 1 cup dairy sour cream
 1 egg
 1 teaspoon ground nutmeg
 ¾ teaspoon baking soda
 ⅓ cup chopped nuts

Grease oblong baking dish, 12 x 7½ x 2 inches. Mix flour, brown sugar and margarine until crumbly. Reserve 1 cup of the mixture for topping.

Stir sour cream, egg, nutmeg and baking soda into remaining crumb mixture just until moistened. Spread evenly in baking dish; sprinkle with reserved crumb mixture and the nuts.

Microwave uncovered 5 minutes; turn dish one-half turn. Microwave until wooden pick inserted near center comes out clean, 3½ to 4½ minutes; cool thoroughly.

PEANUT BUTTER STREUSEL CAKE

 1 package (16 ounces) pound cake mix
 ¼ cup packed brown sugar
 2 tablespoons crunchy peanut butter
    Peanut Butter Frosting (right)

Grease bottom only of square baking dish, 8 x 8 x 2 inches. Mix ⅓ cup cake mix (dry), the brown sugar and peanut butter until crumbly. Prepare remaining cake mix as directed on package except—decrease water by 2 tablespoons. Pour about ⅔ of the batter into baking dish; sprinkle with peanut butter mixture. Swirl lightly with knife. Spoon on remaining batter, spreading to cover.

Microwave uncovered 5 minutes; turn dish one-quarter turn. Microwave until wooden pick inserted in center comes out clean, 2 to 4 minutes. (Parts of cake will appear very moist, but

these parts will continue to cook while standing.) Cool thoroughly; frost with Peanut Butter Frosting.

PEANUT BUTTER FROSTING

 1 cup powdered sugar
 3 tablespoons crunchy peanut butter
 ½ teaspoon vanilla
 2 to 3 tablespoons water

Mix powdered sugar and peanut butter. Stir in vanilla. Beat in water, 1 teaspoon at a time, until smooth and of spreading consistency.

APPLESAUCE-RAISIN UPSIDE-DOWN CAKE

 ⅓ cup packed brown sugar
 ¼ cup chopped nuts
 3 tablespoons margarine or butter
 1 package (15 ounces) applesauce-raisin
    cake mix
 1 cup water

Microwave brown sugar, nuts and margarine uncovered in round baking dish, 8 x 1½ inches, until margarine is melted, 1 to 1½ minutes; stir. Microwave uncovered to boiling, 1 to 1½ minutes. Spread evenly in baking dish.

Mix cake mix and water until smooth; pour over nut mixture in baking dish. Microwave uncovered 5 minutes; turn dish one-quarter turn. Microwave until top springs back when touched lightly, 2 to 3 minutes. Immediately invert dish on serving plate. Let dish remain a minute so sauce drizzles over cake. Spread any remaining sauce over cake.

BANANA-TOPPED CAKE

½ package (18.5-ounce size) yellow cake mix (about 2 cups)
¾ cup packed brown sugar
1 cup flaked coconut
⅓ cup chopped nuts
2 tablespoons milk
⅓ cup margarine or butter
2 medium bananas, sliced

Grease bottom only of oblong baking dish, 12 x 7½ x 2 inches. Prepare cake mix for 1 layer as directed on package. Pour batter into baking dish; spread evenly. Microwave uncovered 4 minutes; turn dish one-half turn. Microwave until wooden pick inserted in center comes out clean, 2½ to 3½ minutes. (Parts of the cake will appear very moist, but these parts will continue to cook while standing.) Cool thoroughly.

Mix brown sugar, coconut, nuts and milk in 1-quart casserole or bowl; add margarine. Microwave uncovered 2 minutes; stir. Microwave uncovered until mixture boils and becomes translucent, 1½ to 2 minutes.

Arrange bananas on cake. Spoon coconut topping over bananas, spreading to cover; cool.

SURPRISE CUPCAKES

1 package (14.5 ounces) chocolate almond snack cake mix
⅓ cup peanut butter (optional)
15 large marshmallows

Prepare cake mix as directed on package except—mix batter in bowl. Spoon into paper-lined plastic muffin cups or custard or coffee cups, filling ½ full. Place 1 teaspoon peanut butter in center of each cupcake; top with a marshmallow. Microwave uncovered 5 cups at a time 1½ minutes. Rotate or rearrange cups and microwave until cake is no longer doughy, 30 seconds to 1 minute. Remove from cups; cool slightly.

15 cupcakes.

ROCKY ROAD BROWNIES

2 squares (1 ounce each) unsweetened chocolate
⅓ cup margarine or butter
1 cup sugar
2 eggs
½ teaspoon vanilla
½ cup all-purpose flour
½ teaspoon salt
¼ teaspoon baking powder
Rocky Road Frosting (below)

Grease bottom only of square baking dish, 8 x 8 x 2 inches. Microwave chocolate and margarine uncovered in 2½-quart casserole or bowl until chocolate is softened, 1½ to 2 minutes. Stir until smooth. Mix in sugar, eggs and vanilla. Stir in flour, salt and baking powder. Spread evenly in baking dish.

Microwave uncovered 3 minutes; turn dish one-quarter turn. Microwave until no longer doughy, 2 to 3 minutes. Cool; frost with Rocky Road Frosting. Refrigerate to set frosting, about 30 minutes. Cut into about 2-inch squares.

16 cookies.

ROCKY ROAD FROSTING

3 tablespoons margarine or butter
1 package (6 ounces) semisweet chocolate chips
1 tablespoon milk
1½ cups miniature marshmallows
⅓ cup chopped nuts

Microwave margarine and chocolate chips uncovered in bowl until chips are softened, 1 to 1½ minutes. Stir until smooth. Blend in milk. Stir in marshmallows and nuts until evenly coated.

PEANUT BUTTER ROCKY ROAD

1   package (6 ounces) semisweet chocolate
      chips
1   package (6 ounces) butterscotch chips
½   cup peanut butter
3   cups miniature marshmallows
½   cup salted peanuts

Place chocolate chips, butterscotch chips and peanut butter in 2-quart bowl. Microwave uncovered until softened, 2 to 2½ minutes. Stir until melted and smooth.

Mix in marshmallows and peanuts until evenly coated. Spread in buttered square baking pan, 8 x 8 x 2 inches. Refrigerate until firm, at least 1 hour. Cut into bars, 2x1 inch.

32 bars.

CHOCOLATE CHIP SQUARES

½   cup packed brown sugar
½   cup margarine or butter, softened
1   egg
1   teaspoon vanilla
½   cup all-purpose flour
½   cup rolled oats
1   teaspoon baking powder
¼   teaspoon salt
⅓   cup semisweet chocolate chips
¼   cup chopped nuts

Grease bottom only of square baking dish, 8 x 8 x 2 inches. Mix brown sugar, margarine, egg and vanilla. Stir in flour, oats, baking powder and salt. Spread evenly in baking dish. Sprinkle with chocolate chips and nuts.

Microwave uncovered 4 minutes; turn dish one-quarter turn. Microwave until no longer doughy, 2 to 3 minutes. Cool; cut into about 2-inch squares.

16 cookies.

FROSTED LEMON TREATS

½   cup margarine or butter, softened
¼   cup sugar
1   egg
¾   teaspoon grated lemon peel
½   teaspoon vanilla
3   tablespoons milk
1¼   cups all-purpose flour
½   teaspoon baking powder
      Lemon Frosting (below)

Grease bottom only of oblong baking dish, 10 x 6 x 1½ inches. Mix margarine, sugar, egg, lemon peel, vanilla and milk. Stir in flour and baking powder. Spread evenly in baking dish.

Microwave uncovered 2 minutes; turn dish one-half turn. Microwave until no longer doughy, 1 to 2 minutes. Cool; frost with Lemon Frosting. Cut into bars, about 2 x 1½ inches.

18 cookies.

LEMON FROSTING

3   tablespoons margarine or butter, softened
¾   cup powdered sugar
¼   teaspoon grated lemon peel
1   teaspoon lemon juice

Beat all ingredients until smooth.

FRUIT-CEREAL CLUSTERS

1   pound white candy coating
1   cup chopped dried apricots
1   cup chopped dates
2   cups salted peanuts
2   cups corn puff cereal

Break candy coating into pieces in 4-quart casserole or bowl. Microwave uncovered until softened, 4 minutes; stir. Microwave uncovered 1 minute. Stir until smooth. Stir in remaining ingredients until evenly coated. Drop by tablespoonfuls onto waxed paper. Refrigerate until set, 30 minutes to 1 hour.

About 4½ dozen clusters.

CHEWY GRAHAM-COCONUT BARS

1 cup packed brown sugar
½ cup margarine or butter, softened
1 egg
¼ teaspoon vanilla
¾ cup all-purpose flour
¾ cup graham cracker crumbs
   (about 9 squares)
⅓ cup flaked coconut
¼ cup chopped nuts
¼ teaspoon salt

Grease bottom only of oblong baking dish, 12 x 7½ x 2 inches. Mix brown sugar, margarine, egg and vanilla. Stir in flour, graham cracker crumbs, coconut, nuts and salt. Spread evenly in baking dish.

Microwave uncovered 3 minutes; turn dish one-half turn. Microwave until wooden pick inserted in center comes out clean, 2 to 3 minutes. (Parts of dough will appear very moist, but these parts will continue to cook while standing.) Cool thoroughly; cut into bars, about 2 x 1 ½ inches.

30 cookies.

PEANUT BUTTER BARS

¾ cup packed brown sugar
½ cup margarine or butter, softened
⅓ cup crunchy peanut butter
1 egg
1 teaspoon vanilla
1 cup all-purpose flour
¾ cup rolled oats
¼ teaspoon salt
   Peanut Butter Frosting (below)

Grease bottom only of oblong baking dish, 12 x 7½ x 2 inches. Mix brown sugar, margarine, peanut butter, egg and vanilla; stir in flour, oats and salt. Spread evenly in baking dish.

Microwave uncovered 3 minutes; turn dish one-half turn. Microwave until no longer doughy, 2 to 3 minutes. Cool; frost with Peanut Butter Frosting. If desired, refrigerate to set frosting. Cut into bars, about 2 x 1½ inches.

30 cookies.

PEANUT BUTTER FROSTING

⅓ cup crunchy peanut butter
1 package (6 ounces) butterscotch chips

Microwave peanut butter and butterscotch chips uncovered until softened, 1 to 1½ minutes. Stir until blended.

SOUPS, SANDWICHES AND SNACKS

POTATO SOUP

    4 slices bacon
    1 medium onion, chopped
    ½ cup water
    1 package (12 ounces) frozen shredded
       hash brown potatoes
  1 ½ teaspoons salt
    ⅛ teaspoon pepper
    3 tablespoons margarine or butter (optional)
    2 tablespoons flour
    2 cups milk
    1 cup water

Place bacon in 2½-quart casserole. Cover with paper towel and microwave until crisp, 4 to 5 minutes. Remove bacon from fat; drain bacon on paper towels.

Add onion to bacon fat. Cover and microwave until onion is tender, 3 to 4 minutes.

Add ½ cup water and the frozen potatoes. Cover and microwave until potatoes are thawed, 6 to 7 minutes.

Stir in salt, pepper and margarine. Shake flour and milk in tightly covered jar; stir into potato mixture with 1 cup water. Cover and microwave 5 minutes; stir. Cover and microwave until mixture boils and thickens slightly, 3 to 5 minutes. Crumble bacon and sprinkle over top.

5 or 6 servings.

ASPARAGUS-CHEESE CHOWDER

    2 cups cubed potatoes (about 2 medium)
    ½ cup sliced carrot
    ½ cup sliced celery
    1 small onion, chopped
    ½ cup water
    2 cups milk
    ¼ cup all-purpose flour
  1 ½ teaspoons salt
    ¼ teaspoon pepper
    ¼ cup margarine or butter
    1 can (15 ounces) cut asparagus
    1 cup shredded Swiss cheese (about
       4 ounces)

Place potatoes, carrot, celery, onion and water in 3-quart casserole. Cover and microwave until vegetables are tender, 10 to 12 minutes.

Shake milk, flour, salt and pepper in tightly covered jar; stir into vegetables. Add margarine. Cover and microwave 3½ minutes; stir. Cover and microwave to boiling, 2 to 3 minutes.

Stir in asparagus (with liquid) and cheese. Cover and microwave until hot and bubbly and cheese is melted, 3 to 4 minutes. Stir.

5 or 6 servings.

CORN-HAM CHOWDER

  1 can (11 ounces) condensed Cheddar
     cheese soup
  2 cups water
  1 can (10¾ ounces) condensed cream of
     potato soup
  1 can (17 ounces) cream-style corn
1½ cups cubed cooked ham
  1 teaspoon chopped chives
 ¼ teaspoon dry mustard

Stir water gradually into cheese soup in 2½-quart casserole until smooth; stir in remaining ingredients. Cover and microwave 8 minutes; stir. Cover and microwave until hot and bubbly, 4 to 6 minutes; stir.

5 or 6 servings.

ZUCCHINI SOUP

  2 tablespoons margarine or butter
  1 small onion, chopped
  4 cups sliced zucchini (about 1 pound)
  1 can (10¾ ounces) condensed cream of
     chicken soup
  2 cups water
  1 teaspoon salt
 ½ teaspoon dried basil leaves
 ⅛ teaspoon pepper

Place margarine, onion and zucchini in 2-quart casserole. Cover and microwave until vegetables are tender, 9 to 11 minutes.

Place soup, 1 cup of the water and the zucchini mixture in blender container. Cover and blend on medium-high speed until smooth, about 1 minute.

Return mixture to casserole. Stir in remaining 1 cup water, the salt, basil and pepper. Cover and microwave until hot and bubbly, 8 to 10 minutes. (Can be refrigerated and served cold.)

4 servings.

BEAN AND WIENER SOUP

 ½ cup chopped green pepper
  1 small onion, chopped
  2 tablespoons margarine or butter
  1 can (11½ ounces) condensed bean with
     bacon soup
1⅓ cups water
  2 tablespoons catsup
 ½ teaspoon Worcestershire sauce
 ½ teaspoon prepared mustard
  4 frankfurters, sliced

Place green pepper, onion and margarine in 1½-quart casserole. Cover and microwave until onion is tender, 4 to 5 minutes.

Stir in remaining ingredients. Cover and microwave 4 minutes; stir. Cover and microwave until hot and bubbly, 2 to 3 minutes.

3 or 4 servings.

BEER-CHEESE SOUP

 ¼ cup margarine or butter
  1 small onion, chopped
 ⅓ cup all-purpose flour
  1 tablespoon instant chicken bouillon
3½ cups milk
  1 jar (8 ounces) pasteurized process
     cheese spread
  1 cup shredded Cheddar cheese
     (about 4 ounces)
  1 cup beer

Place margarine and onion in 2-quart casserole. Cover and microwave until onion is tender, 3 to 4 minutes. Stir in flour and bouillon, then gradually stir in milk. Cover and microwave 6 minutes; stir. Cover and microwave to boiling, 3 to 5 minutes.

Stir in cheese spread, cheese and beer. Cover and microwave until hot and bubbly and cheese is melted 3 to 4 minutes; stir.

5 or 6 servings.

FISH GUMBO

2 tablespoons margarine or butter
⅓ cup sliced green onions
½ cup chopped celery
1 can (10¾ ounces) condensed tomato soup
1 can (10¾ ounces) condensed cream of shrimp soup
1 can (14½ ounces) stewed tomatoes
1 can (14¼ ounces) cut okra
1 tablespoon dry white wine (optional)
1 bay leaf
1 pound fish fillets, cut into 1-inch pieces

Place margarine, onions and celery in 3-quart casserole. Cover and microwave until vegetables are tender, 3 to 4 minutes.

Mix in soups, canned vegetables (with liquid), wine and bay leaf. Cover and microwave to boiling, 8 to 10 minutes.

Stir in fish. Cover and microwave 4 minutes; stir. Cover and microwave until fish flakes easily with a fork, 2 to 3 minutes.

6 servings.

HOT CHICKEN SALAD SANDWICHES

1½ cups cut-up cooked chicken
½ cup chopped celery
¼ cup chopped almonds or pecans
⅓ cup drained crushed pineapple
¼ cup mayonnaise or salad dressing
4 English muffins, split and toasted
  Avocado slices (optional)

Mix chicken, celery, almonds, pineapple and mayonnaise. Place muffins cut sides up on serving plate. Spread chicken mixture onto muffin halves, being careful to bring to edges.

Microwave uncovered until filling is warm, 1¼ to 2 minutes. Garnish with avocado slices.

4 servings.

HAM AND CHEESE WITH COLESLAW

2 tablespoons margarine or butter
½ teaspoon prepared mustard
4 slices rye bread, toasted
4 slices cooked ham
1 large tomato, sliced
4 slices cheese
1 cup coleslaw

Microwave margarine uncovered in custard cup until softened, 15 to 30 seconds. Blend in mustard. Spread margarine on one side of each toast slice. Place slices buttered sides up on serving plate; top with ham, tomato and cheese slices.

Microwave uncovered until cheese begins to melt, 1½ to 2 minutes. Top each sandwich with a spoonful of coleslaw.

4 sandwiches.

BACON, CHEESE AND TOMATO SANDWICHES

3 slices bacon
3 slices rye bread, toasted
2 tablespoons mayonnaise or salad dressing
½ teaspoon dried dill weed
1 large tomato, sliced
3 slices Swiss cheese

Place bacon between layers of paper towels on glass plate. Microwave until crisp, 2½ to 3½ minutes.

Spread toast with mayonnaise; sprinkle with dill. Place toast slices on serving plate; top with tomato and cheese slices. Crumble bacon and sprinkle over top.

Microwave uncovered until cheese begins to melt, 1 to 1½ minutes.

3 sandwiches.

SLOPPY FRANKS

 1 small onion, chopped
⅓ cup chopped green pepper
 1 tablespoon margarine or butter
½ cup barbecue sauce
¼ cup catsup
 1 pound frankfurters, cut into ¼-inch slices
12 hamburger buns, split

Place onion, green pepper and margarine in 1-quart casserole. Cover and microwave until vegetables are tender, 3 to 4 minutes.

Stir in barbecue sauce, catsup and frankfurters. Cover and microwave 2½ minutes; stir. Cover and microwave until mixture boils, 2 to 3 minutes.

Spoon mixture into buns on serving plate. Microwave uncovered until buns are hot, 1 to 2 minutes.

12 sandwiches.

CHILI DOGS

 2 frankfurters
 2 frankfurter buns, split
⅓ cup chili with beans

Microwave frankfurters uncovered until warm, 30 to 45 seconds. Place 1 frankfurter in each bun; spoon chili onto frankfurters. Microwave uncovered until chili is hot, 1 to 1½ minutes.

2 sandwiches.

NOTE: If preparing just one chili dog, microwave uncovered 30 to 45 seconds.

HOBO BUNS

 2 tablespoons mayonnaise or salad dressing
½ teaspoon prepared mustard
 3 Kaiser or French rolls, split
 3 slices bologna
 1 large tomato, sliced
 3 green pepper rings
 3 slices cheese

Mix mayonnaise and mustard; spread over cut sides of rolls. Place bottom halves of rolls on paper napkins. Top with bologna, tomato, green pepper, cheese and top halves of rolls.

Microwave uncovered until cheese begins to melt, 1 to 1½ minutes.

3 sandwiches.

BARBECUED BEEF ON BUNS

 1 cup catsup
 2 tablespoons brown sugar
 1 tablespoon lemon juice
 1 tablespoon Worcestershire sauce
 1 teaspoon prepared mustard
½ teaspoon onion salt
⅛ teaspoon pepper
 8 ounces thinly sliced cooked roast beef (8 to 10 slices)
 4 hamburger buns, split

Mix catsup, brown sugar, lemon juice, Worcestershire sauce, mustard, onion salt and pepper in 2-cup glass measure. Microwave 1½ minutes; stir. Microwave to boiling, 1 to 2 minutes.

Layer half of the beef slices and half of the sauce in 1-quart casserole; repeat. Cover and microwave until hot and bubbly, 1½ to 2½ minutes.

Place bottom halves of buns on paper serving plate. Top with beef and remaining bun halves. Microwave uncovered until buns are hot, 30 seconds to 1 minute.

4 sandwiches.

TUNA BUNS

2 hard-cooked eggs, chopped
1 can (6½ ounces) tuna, drained
1 package (4 ounces) shredded Cheddar
  cheese (about 1 cup)
¼ cup chopped green pepper
2 tablespoons finely chopped onion
½ teaspoon prepared mustard
½ cup mayonnaise or salad dressing
6 to 8 hamburger buns, split

Mix eggs, tuna, cheese, green pepper, onion, mustard and mayonnaise. Fill buns with tuna mixture. Place on paper serving plate.

Microwave uncovered until filling is warm, 1½ to 2 minutes.

6 to 8 sandwiches.

STORE-AND-SPOON BURGERS

1 pound hamburger
¼ cup catsup
4 teaspoons prepared mustard
½ teaspoon salt
  Dash of pepper
½ cup shredded process cheese (2 ounces)
8 hamburger buns, split

Crumble hamburger into 1-quart casserole. Microwave uncovered 4 minutes. Stir to break up meat. Microwave uncovered until meat is firm, 1 to 2 minutes; drain.

Stir in catsup, mustard, salt, pepper and cheese. Cover and refrigerate until ready to serve (can be stored up to 3 days).

To serve, spoon about ¼ cup meat mixture between bun halves. Microwave uncovered on paper plates or napkins until filling is hot:

  1 bun — 15 to 30 seconds
  2 buns — 30 to 45 seconds
  4 buns — 1 to 1½ minutes

8 sandwiches.

PIZZA BURGERS

1 pound hamburger
1 can (6 ounces) tomato paste
½ cup finely chopped pepperoni
1 slice bread, crumbled
1 teaspoon salt
½ teaspoon dried oregano leaves
  Dash of pepper
1 egg, beaten
  Sliced olives or onion or green pepper rings
1 cup shredded mozzarella cheese (about 4
  ounces)
8 hamburger buns, split

Mix hamburger, half of the tomato paste, the pepperoni, bread, salt, oregano, pepper and egg. Shape into 8 patties. Place in oblong baking dish, 12 x 7½ x 2 inches. Cover loosely and microwave 6 minutes; turn dish one-half turn. Microwave until meat is firm, 4 to 5 minutes.

Spread cut sides of buns with remaining tomato paste. Place bottom halves of buns on paper serving plate. Place a patty on each bun half. Top with olives, cheese and top half of bun. Microwave uncovered until cheese begins to melt, 1½ to 2 minutes.

8 sandwiches.

BANANA-PEANUT BUTTER BUNS

2 frankfurter buns, split and buttered
¼ cup peanut butter
1 banana

Spread buns with peanut butter. Cut banana lengthwise in half; place 1 half in each bun.

Microwave uncovered until filling is hot, 30 seconds to 1 minute.

2 sandwiches.

CARAMEL CORN

16 cups popped corn
 1 cup packed brown sugar
½ cup margarine or butter
¼ cup light corn syrup
½ teaspoon salt
½ teaspoon baking soda

Divide popped corn between two 4-quart bowls.

Mix brown sugar, margarine, corn syrup and salt in 2½-quart casserole. Microwave uncovered 2½ minutes; stir. Microwave uncovered to boiling, 30 seconds. Boil 3 minutes.

Stir in baking soda. Pour syrup mixture on popped corn, stirring until mixed. Microwave uncovered, one bowl at a time, until well coated, 2½ to 3½ minutes, stirring every minute. Cool, stirring occasionally.

16 cups caramel corn.

COOKED CARAMEL-APPLE SLICES

2 caramels
1 medium apple, sliced

Place a caramel in each of 2 small serving dishes. Divide apple slices between dishes. Microwave uncovered until apple is tender, 2 to 3 minutes. Stir to coat apple slices with caramel. Serve warm.

2 snacks.

GRAHAM-FRUIT PUFFS

Top graham cracker squares with banana or apple slices. Place squares on paper napkins or paper towels. Top each square with a large marshmallow. Microwave until marshmallow is puffed:

1 or 2 puffs—15 to 30 seconds
3 or 4 puffs—30 to 45 seconds

Top each puff with another cracker square.

NOTE: For extra heartiness, spread crackers with peanut butter before topping with fruit slices.

QUICK CHEESE FONDUE

1 can (11 ounces) condensed Cheddar cheese soup
¼ cup dry white wine
 Dash of garlic powder
⅛ teaspoon Worcestershire sauce
½ cup shredded Swiss or Cheddar cheese (about 2 ounces)
 French bread, cut into 1-inch cubes

Mix soup, wine, garlic powder and Worcestershire sauce in 1-quart casserole. Cover and microwave 2½ minutes.

Stir in cheese. Microwave uncovered until mixture is smooth, 2½ to 3 minutes, stirring every minute. If desired, pour into fondue pot or chafing dish to keep warm. Use long-handled forks to spear bread cubes, then dip and swirl in fondue with a stirring motion.

4 or 5 servings.

STORE 'N HEAT CHEESE SPREAD

1 jar (2½ ounces) dried beef
1 cup water
1 package (8 ounces) cream cheese
¼ cup mayonnaise or salad dressing
¼ cup chopped green onions
2 teaspoons dried parsley flakes
2 cups shredded Cheddar cheese
    (about 8 ounces)
    Assorted crackers
    Chopped nuts (optional)

Snip beef into small pieces. Combine beef and water in 2-cup glass measure. Microwave to boiling, 2 to 3 minutes; drain.

Microwave cream cheese uncovered until softened, 30 to 45 seconds. Mix in beef, mayonnaise, green onions, parsley and cheese. Cover tightly and refrigerate up to 1 week.

To serve, spread a rounded tablespoonful of cheese mixture on each cracker; sprinkle with nuts. Place about 15 to 20 crackers on serving plate. Microwave until spread is warm, 30 seconds to 1 minute.

About 2½ cups spread.

NOTE: Spread can be divided in half and formed into 2 rolls about 12 inches long. Roll in nuts; wrap tightly and refrigerate. To serve, cut spread into ⅝-inch slices and place on crackers. Microwave as directed above.

FILLED TORTILLA SNACKS

⅔ cup chili with beans
2 flour tortillas
¼ cup shredded mozzarella cheese

Spoon chili down center of each tortilla; sprinkle with cheese. Fold sides of tortilla up over filling, overlapping edges. Microwave uncovered until filling is hot, 1 to 1½ minutes.

2 snacks.

NOTE: If preparing just one tortilla, microwave 30 to 45 seconds.

MICROWAVE BEEF JERKY

1 pound boneless beef round steak
1½ teaspoons salt
⅛ teaspoon pepper
1 teaspoon liquid smoke

Trim fat from meat; discard. Cut steak across the grain into ⅛-inch strips, about 5 inches long.

Layer ⅓ each of the meat, salt, pepper and liquid smoke in loaf pan, 9 x 5 x 3 inches; repeat 2 times. Cover tightly and refrigerate at least 8 hours.

Arrange about ⅓ of the meat strips on microwave roasting rack in oblong baking dish, 12 x 7½ x 2 inches. Cover with paper towel and microwave 7 minutes; turn strips. Cover and microwave until crisp, 2 to 3 minutes. Repeat with remaining meat.

8 to 10 servings.

NOTE: If you don't have a roasting rack, place strips on paper plate.

INDEX